A Working Class Alternative To Labour

1

A Working Class Alternative To Labour

A Working Class Alternative To Labour

By Gregory Motton

Levellers Press

A Working Class Alternative To Labour
First published 2013
by Levellers Press
2 Middle Street,
Deal CT14 7AG
levellerspress@yahoo.co.uk

ISBN 978-0-9564364-4-3

Printed in England by Orbital Print Ltd.

"Above all things good policy is to be used so that the treasures and monies in a state be not gathered into a few hands... Money is like fertilizer, not good except it be spread."
Francis Bacon *Of Seditions and Troubles.*

A Working Class Alternative To Labour

A Larger Slice Of The Pie.
A proposal for a more equal society.

"It can only get better". Well, did it?

Does anyone still remember the song they played at the party on the night of the great Labour victory of 1997? "It Can Only Get Better" by D.Ream.

In 1979 there were 7.6 million people living on less than 60% of the median income. By 1997 it had gone up to 14 million, (that's 22% of the population) and has stayed around that ever since. It went down slightly to 13 million after 10 years of Labour government. But the number of people on *very low incomes,* that is 40% of the median, was 1.3 million in 1979, (2.9% of the population), went up to 5 million in 1997, and stayed at that through the Labour government, and is now at 5.9 million (9.8% of the population).

 (Source: Joseph Rowantree Foundation, Poverty and Wealth Across Britain 2007).

We have a higher relative poverty level than the average in Europe, only a handful of other EU members are behind us, Greece, Italy, Spain, Latvia, Romania and Bulgaria.

At the other end of the scale: In 1975 the top 1% of Britons owned 6.1% of all the wealth. By 2005 they owned 21% *(Source:Her Majesty's Revenue and Customs)*.

In 1975 the top 10% of Britons owned 27% of all the wealth, by 2005 they owned 53% and still do *(Source:Office of National Statistics)*, and they get 40% of all the *income (Source: Institute of Fiscal Studies)*.

Here is a list showing how much the top 10% own in other countries for comparison:
UK 53%
Sweden 22%
Germany 22%
Spain 26%
Russia 31%
Finland 22%
South Africa 51%
China 31%
India 28%
USA 29%

(Source: United Nations)

In Britain, the *incomes* of the top 10% are more than the incomes of the all the bottom 50% put together.

"The top 0.1% get 4.3% of all income - the highest figure in the UK since the 1930s, and three times as much as they received as a share of income in 1979"*(Source: Institute of Fiscal Studies)*.

8

We are used to reading these sorts of figures, we accept them, like we accept the weather.

Why is Britain still like this?

How did it happen that despite two successive Labour landslides giving them a massive majority in the House of Commons, they failed to reverse or even halt the move towards greater inequality? Why, despite the efforts of a Labour Chancellor who strove to alleviate child poverty by expanding the Family Income Supplement into Working Family Tax Credits, a pretty generous help for the low paid in work, did not only child poverty stay with us, but the rich continue to get richer in relation to the rest of us, while the poorest of the working classes remain permanently poor? And how did it happen that the middle classes benefited so much more than the working classes from a Labour government? "The gap between middle incomes and low incomes has increased substantially over the past ten years" *(Source: Poverty.org. - Department of Works and Pensions).*

Why didn't Labour use their great majority to rid Britain of poverty, or to advance the working class struggle for a larger slice of the wages pie?

Part of the answer is perhaps that the working class struggle *for greater pay* which is what it was in the early days of the union movement, became subsumed by a notion of *the state* as the major player in the redistribution of wealth. Gordon Brown came from that tradition, and strove within it to alleviate poverty in the way he knew how. But the role given to the state has always tended to benefit the bureaucratic and political classes, as their importance and their material advantages and employment grows, (28% of the workforce work in government, more than work in manufacture and construction) - and has left a large part of the working classes still, as ever, on low pay, and in poverty. The working class struggle needs to find representation in a move for higher pay. The state shouldn't need to be presiding over handouts to make up for low pay. It's time the working classes got a fair share of the pie.

The Need To Reverse The Trickle-*Up* Economy - To Move Money From the Top to the Bottom

At Present We have a Trickle-Up Economy; The money trickles up to the top - then leaves the country.

LOOK AT ANY BRITISH HIGH STREET, AT THE chain stores that dominate. It doesn't just tell the story of the difficulty for smaller retailers to afford the inflated rents for shops, or of the deliberate and systematic way the chains seek to put smaller shops out of business. No, it tells a wider story of an economy where increasingly all the money ends up where money already is, at the top, while it is harder and harder for anyone else to make any profit at all. But this effect goes further than simply increasing the gulf between rich and poor in Britain. It creates a *national* poverty into which we are blindly falling, led by the smiling family-friendly face of the retail outlets of the corporations. For the chains themselves are not self owned, but belong to other corporations and banks. These take the profits and invest them where growth is quickest, abroad, in developing nations and in Europe. In 2011 British companies invested £68bn abroad, one third of all profits *(Source: HM Treasury)*. The most telling symptom is that almost everything on the shelves in the shops is made abroad. A country like Britain finds itself increasingly "redundant", surplus to the needs of the corporations that live upon its body, like ticks, and then drop off and move away, taking its life blood with them, the profit earned by the people there. Because of banks' investment abroad, and because such a large proportion of the profit made in our economy is made by giant corporations, (in retailing for example, the 4 big stores have 80% of the market share), and because they often pay low wages, money made here does not go round and round in our economy spreading prosperity; fully one third of it leaves the country and takes prosperity with it.

The result here is that we all become not a nation of shopkeepers any more, but a nation of low paid employees, getting poorer and poorer. Eventually we will be wrapping German and Chinese goods, a source of cheap labour.

Keeping wages low while producing less and less and importing what we use, is a sure way to long term poverty and decline. £30bn, by far the largest single portion of the £68bn British companies invest abroad, goes to Europe; and we import most, not from China, but from Germany.

The Low Wage Economy

Somewhere along the road the struggle to get a larger slice of the pie for the low paid lost its way - the idea seems almost to have been forgotten by the major political parties.

Low wages have been presented as a means of competing with overseas producers. It isn't. The low wage economy is largely merely an unequal distribution of the wages bill, and quite simply an unfair distribution between wages and profit, with little or no effect on competition abroad. The reason is that we don't compete with low grade manufactures produced by cheap labour. Our fields of exports compete, often unfavourably, with for example, Germany and Sweden who pay themselves high wages. Low pay can be about competition between rival domestic firms (if it is about competition at all). In fact, low pay has a negative effect on British companies competing abroad; 1) It leaves more profit for large corporations investing abroad in foreign companies 2) It creates a weak domestic market for British goods which means they lack a springboard for exports. In a recent set of Treasury figures, for example, wages had fallen by 3.5%, and so had exports. Most of the low paid in Britain are not involved in the production of exports. No, rather they are involved in producing profits that can be invested in foreign companies.

Where are the low paid jobs? - Not in export industries as the list below shows:

Retail 2,682,000
Hotels, Catering 1, 689,000

Social Care 638,000
Employment Agencies 625,000
Cleaning 619,000
Leisure, travel, sport 485,000
Food processing 325,000
Agriculture 203,000
Security 174,000
Hairdressing 84,000
Textiles 79,000

Total 8,040,000

(Source: Office of National Statistics, doesn't include self employed and family workers, and government training schemes)

Greater equality of wages is inevitable - the only question is how long does it have to take? It is inevitable and common sense requires it. There is simply no good reason, either moral or economic, why 30% of the population should have hardly enough to get by on while others, who work no harder than they do, get more than they can spend. Poverty is something we are choosing to keep, it is a drain on the economy, it is unnecessary and expensive, and it keeps the country poor. If it is supposed to make British exports more competitive then it clearly hasn't worked, as our manufacturing exports shrank in the 1980s and have never recovered. Exports have shrunk during the period of low wages. Low wages do not benefit the export industries because quite simply they are not usually the ones paying low wages. Low wages benefit chiefly the large retailers whose profits are kept high by the invidious practice. The profits go to the shareholders, themselves large corporations, not individuals. The corporations which own everything are getting bigger and bigger, and **the money they own benefits our society less and less**. The "trickle down", promised by Thatcher, never materialised, as we have the opposite, a **trickle up** economy, where wealth is consolidated in the hands of progressively fewer, larger bodies. It is a simple choice we are making as a society to keep 8 million poor, while nameless (unknown to most) organisations, take what the low paid have generated through their work. How long are we going to accept such a sordid arrangement? When are we going to have the dignity and common sense to share out the material wealth more fairly? When are even the middle classes going to tire of living in a society where the social cost of poverty is all around them?

Is it right that the tax payer should subsidise low paying employers though benefits, housing benefit, and other costs of poverty which the low wage economy results in?

It is as if we are sleepwalking in our acceptance of what is an entirely unnecessary blight upon our national life. The two major parties know about it and do nothing, except, within the limited scope of their imaginations, to look after the poor, through benefits and other piecemeal measures. But neither of them seem to consider getting rid of poverty by sharing out the money - by ensuring significantly higher wages for the lowest paid workers.

A minimum wage at 80% of the median*, and unemployment benefit above the poverty line.

(See Appendix for how the exact figure was arrived at)

If the minimum wage was raised so that all workers were paid the same as the lower middle classes, £9.30 per hour which is £19,400 pa, (London £11.38phr £23,670pa) and if unemployment benefit* was raised to a level somewhere about 20% below that, then there would eventually be an end to poverty in Britain for millions of people.

*The current job seekers allowance is set at £64 per week, which is 50% of the government's own poverty safety line for adults *(Source: Joseph Rowantree Foundation, HM Treasury).*

Benefits aren't too high, wages are too low.

For the unemployed poor, the difference between being unemployed and getting a job is not enough, because jobs are so low paid. Because wages are so low, getting a job when you are poor does not mean your troubles are over. It is necessary for any mature society to realise the level of hopelessness that fact brings to anyone suffering long term unemployment. We are used to thinking, mistakenly, that unemployment benefit it too high, the "benefits trap" as it is known. In fact the lack of incentive to get work lies in the low wages.

The dreadful social cost of generations of grinding poverty - the misery, the crime, the degradation, the violence, the abuse, the ignorance and the suffering, would eventually lose its grip upon the millions among us who suffer this man-made blight; the ugliness, the depressing run-down decline that haunts many British towns, would eventually disappear, as people were paid enough to take control of their own lives, to invest in their improvement and betterment of their conditions.

It would also provide a more healthy domestic market as a basis for the revival of British industry - which is essential if we are to avert long term national decline into poor nation status.

Why haven't we, why don't we, take the simple and obvious step to clear away the awful waste of poverty and its endless and hideous consequences? Why do we fiddle and tinker with inadequate measures to ameliorate the plague instead of simply giving people the means to cure it immediately themselves - better pay; A proper wage that leaves **a surplus** at the end of the month; The surplus that the middle classes have that enables them to live full lives and invest in their children's futures. The working classes, who are not paid that kind of amount, do actually produce that amount and much more, but it is taken by their employers, as profit. A fair wage would return that surplus to the ones who earnt it, so that we *all* can benefit in the same way, so that we *all* can afford to live decent and civilised lives, and to reach our potentials.

What would unemployment benefit at that level cost?

Besides roughly £5bn on Job-Seekers Allowance, government spends large amounts to support the poor out of work and in work.

While it would cost maybe £20bn to put employment benefits (Job Seekers Allowance) up to 80% of the suggested minimum wage, that increase along with the suggested minimum wage itself would replace a large proportion of government payments on supporting the out of work.

£17bn on Housing Benefit

£5bn on Council Tax Benefit

£7bn on Income Support.

Some of this, and other benefits, are paid to the poor *in work*.

More tax is not the answer

The Labour solution to poverty has always been tax. In fact it was Gordon Brown's spending on benefits to alleviate poverty without increasing wages, that put us into a budget deficit from 2002 onwards. Middle class Labourites profess their willingness to "pay more tax" as some kind of proof of their commitment to equality. The test however is if they will support real equality brought about by higher wages for the lower paid.

We have seen over the past 80 years or so, how tax is of only limited use as a wealth redistributor. If it worked on its own, it would have worked by now, if it worked without higher wages, there wouldn't be the glaring inequalities we have today. One side effect of using tax on its own, is that it creates a huge bureaucracy - a well paid middle class one of course. And bureaucracies tend to feed upon the beast they live on, and transform its function to feed their own need to continue to grow. In other words the bureaucracy has the power to shape society to suit its own needs and beliefs.

Maynard Keynes' solution to the depression of the 1930s was for government to stimulate the economy by spending on works, on the superstructure, roads etc. This was spreading money out in the economy by spending money that had been raised as tax. It brought 25 years of prosperity to Britain, Europe and the United States where his theories were adopted after the war, and brought also some improvement in working class wages, largely because of high employment levels and the rise in wages that brings. But when this policy came to an end in the mid 1970s, then those gains were lost, and then reversed, as the figures on pages 1 and 2 show. The working class share of the pie shrank. The moment for a significant and final reallocation of wealth had been missed, partly because there was not a specific attempt made to share out the wealth through wages, through a claim on profits.

Why should government gather tax to spend money to stimulate the economy when there is still a need for more money as wages? Giving people sufficient wages so that they can spend it themselves is another way of putting money in the economy, a more direct way as it by-passes the Treasury. Money spent by government during the Keynesian period did go into wages, but where did the money come from in the first place? - Wages. Income tax, as opposed to Corporation Tax, is a tax on work, not on profits. And only 25% of government revenue comes from Corporation Tax, on profits. In other words, 75% of wages generated by government spending, is merely workers paying themselves back the tax they have paid, and working for the privilege.

Putting money into the economy by insisting on higher wages, money that is otherwise leaving it through outward investment, addresses the fundamental problem of inequality of wealth.

Opponents to government attempts to redistribute wealth through tax, and the nationalisation of industries, call it confiscation. But if people simply insist on higher wages, and make sure it comes from the profits, - that can hardly be called confiscation, it is what it is; a claim on the profits they have created by their own labour. It is harder to argue against. It might also be harder to reverse.

Isn't there a good reason why we have kept poverty in Britain?

Surely we have kept the nightmare of poverty for some good sound economic reason? Well, no. On the contrary, poverty is bad for the economy, it is a self inflicted impediment to overall growth and prosperity. Removing it would not *cost* anything, it would generate wealth not reduce it.

Where would the money come from to pay everyone a fair wage? -

It would cost roughly £30bn to put up the wages of the low paid to around £19,000 pa. Double that amount is invested abroad each year, from companies' profits.

So, it wouldn't come from government, not from taxes (except for public employees of course). Everyone's wages make up part of the wages bill. Whatever is not paid in wages and other costs is left as profit. To pay the currently low paid 80% of the average wage, would require either the current wages bill to be shared out differently, (i.e. more evenly), or for some of the *profits* to be spent on wages. Ideally it would be taken first from the largest pile, the profits or the *high* wages piles. In this book the focus is on the profits as the likely source of the money. It would come from the profits of the low pay employers. And where do they get their profits? It is the product of the labour of their employees. This is about workers taking back a larger percentage of what they earn for their employers. People ask where the money is to come from, as if wealth starts its life in the pockets of the rich. It doesn't. Wealth is created by the labour of many working hands.

A girl working on a checkout receives maybe £7 per hour, but she earns twice that amount of profit for the company.

Tesco for example, the biggest private sector employer, employs 260,000 workers on £15,000 or more. To increase those to £19,000 (although not *all* of those are on below £9.30phr) would cost them £1bn, one third of Tesco's profits. That money would otherwise go into the banks, whence apart from hedge funds, futures and derivatives, much of it is invested into foreign companies, sowing the seeds of future decline for our own. Putting money into the economy as wages by-passes the large investment banks.

Where does the profit go other than to Tesco's bank account? It goes to the shareholders? Who are they?

Eighty-nine per cent of Tesco is owned by corporations, of those the larger ones are;

FMR Corporation and Fidelity Intl. Ltd. (a multinational financial services corporation) which has invested £396,502,547 resulting in a 5.02% shareholding.

Legal and General Group PLC (another multinational financial services company) has invested around £315,905,159 resulting in a 4.00% shareholding.

Barclays has invested £300,460,803 resulting in a 3.80% shareholding.

Capital Group Companies Inc. (an investment management group of companies) has invested £290,054,076 resulting in a 3.65% shareholding *(Source: Tesco PLC).*

And so on.

To find out where *that* money is going, you would need to look up each corporation and see who owns *them*, and so on.

Employers sponging on benefits

After wondering where the money would come to pay for a higher minimum wage, you might also like to ask where the money comes from to pay Housing Benefit and Working Family Tax Credit, which effectively subsidises the employers who pay low wages. The answer? - It comes from the tax payer.

For decades government has been subsidising low wages by housing benefit and other benefits to the low paid. The government spends around £60bn of tax payers' money on <u>in-work</u> benefits *(Source: Dept. of Work and Pensions.)* This hides the problem of low pay - It means effectively the tax payer is giving money to employers to put in their bank accounts, and send out of the country. Low wage employers are the real spongers.

That £60bn of in-work benefits is more than the whole of the yearly debt interest, or over half the NHS budget.

Would a higher minimum wage result in lower wages for everyone else, and/or unemployment?

In the countries where the wages are shared out more fairly, the median wages are far higher than here too, and the unemployment rate is similar or a lot lower. See below:

	UK	Germany	Sweden	Denmark	France	Holland
Monthly ave. wage (£)	346	431	410	608	428	402
Annual trade def/surpl (£)	43bn deficit	142bn **surplus**	24bn **surplus**	9bn **surplus**	46bn deficit	41bn **surplus**
Workers on less than 2/3 of median	21.60%	19.60%	10.00%	8.00%	8.80%	13.90%
Unemployment	7.80%	5.40%	8.80%	4.40%	10.00%	8.20%
Pop (Millions)	62	81.7	9.4	5.5	65	16

The table shows countries with high average wages with unemployment rates similar to, or lower than, the UK, and with healthy trade surpluses.

It is worth noting that neither Germany, Denmark or Sweden have statutory minimum wages. They have not needed them since their trade unions were successful in gaining higher wages for their members. Their wages are set by trade union negotiation. In Britain this has been a failure, and trade unions are widely discredited as a result. In Sweden, for example, higher wages were achieved as part of the programme of reforms by a radical Social Democrat government. At the same time that Sweden was achieving some of the highest wages in Europe, in the 1960s and 70s, the Labour Party was failing to support the unions in Britain, and the result was the strikes and unrest, and eventual collapse of the unions. It would be a slow and almost impossible task politically, to revive the bargaining power of the trade unions at this stage. Trade unions depend for their success on a government that is sympathetic to their purpose of raising wages. Historically governments in Britain, even Labour ones, have failed to give that support, and so advances in wages were immediately clawed back as inflationary price rises by manufacturers and retailers - they simply put up their prices. As regards minimum wages, there is a *de facto* minimum wage in Sweden and Denmark for example, but it is not statutory, but set by the unions. The lowest wages in those countries are far higher than the lowest wages in Britain. It is those higher wages at the bottom end of the scale, that have reformed those societies and eliminated the kind of poverty we have continued to accept in Britain. They have brought social equality that we in Britain can only dream of - until we take action to bring such changes here.

The Living Wage Campaign

There is already a campaign for a Living Wage; it is currently set at £7.45 (£8.10 in London). Most of those who campaign for it feel that it should be voluntary.

Aside from the voluntary aspect, it is simply not enough. It is still based upon an idea of ameliorating the position of the poor, not of changing the class system.

£7.45 per hour, £1291 pcm, £298 per week, £15496 per year is a figure limited by a fear of upsetting the economy.

The campaign for a living wage is not connected to any policies for preventing inflation, such as price control, without which most of the gains of a higher minimum wage would simply be wiped away by deliberately inflationary tactics by capital.

While the campaign for a Living Wage is sometimes associated with ideas about grass roots agitation for generally better conditions, it is not connected to any plans for a return to manufacturing, improving the balance of payments, nor to any idea of changing the fundamental direction of the flow of wealth, from upwards to downwards in our society.

If the Living Wage were adopted by employers tomorrow it would makes peoples lives better, but it would not remove poverty, nor substantially change the inequality in our society.

A Social and Economic Revolution

The figure in this book, £9.30per hour, £372 per week £1612per month, £19,400 per year is based on a hope of transforming the class system.

Some supporters of the Living Wage are afraid of negative impacts even though there is little evidence of their likelihood. Indeed similar fears seemed to argue even against the idea of a *low* minimum wage when it was first introduced here. The truth is that higher wages for the lowest paid do not bring about unemployment in countries where they exist (whether brought about by collective bargaining or minimum wage legislation) for the simple reason that the work needs to be done, the employers need the labour, and they will pay as little or as much as they have to to get the work done. Moving workers around from poor areas to less poor ones has always been a method of keeping wages down. This includes of course immigration, that is what it is for, and that is why the middle classes defend it so passionately and emotively; they know the alternative is that the working classes would demand higher wages to clear their drains and tidy their houses. The European Union tries to ensure that cheap labour from poorer European countries is always available to push down the wages of workers in the richer countries (see the section on the EU below). The effect of *high* minimum wages would be that it would leave less profit. That much is true. The question is, can our society live with companies getting less profit?

It is a matter of deciding what that profit level should be. Working class politics is about making sure that the profit level is part of a general plan for the prosperity of *all* classes of society.

Firstly, can the large corporations live with smaller profits?

The power and size of the Multi National Corporations, including banks and financial institutions of course, is one of the most important political issues of today. It is a threat to democracy and freedom as well as to prosperity, it is even a threat to the rights of property, the cornerstone of capitalism. The Multi National Corporations are a threat to these things by their sheer power to dwarf them and interfere with their functioning. The Multi National Corporations' size and power is such that their ability to permeate and control vital institutions including politics and the media and social and intellectual movements, casts a shadow on the ability of man to first perceive and then truthfully report phenomena, to understand his own situation and to be an agent within it. They are a power in some ways greater than governments and religions. In that, and in the power of their propaganda over the development of ideas, they are an attempt to control the mind, the will and the spirit of man. Together they represent some of the greatest power that has been on earth.

Interestingly too they are of course greater than the individuals within them who ostensibly control them. The rich and powerful may come and go, but the Multi National Corporations remain and grow stronger, invisibly shifting their forms so that their might is incomprehensible to mere mortals, un-namable. In short we don't really know what form they take. The complexity of their natures is far greater than that of the interlocking families of the Age of Kings, easily comprehensible to any genealogist or historian. What would it take to trace the ownership and mode of operating of the nebulous group of entities that are the family of Multi National Corporations? It is not a matter even of tracing and locating and naming the super rich, they are not the most relevant aspect. The question rather is; how are these entities formed and how do they work their effect? Who, if anyone, does control them, or who do the Multi National Corporations control? Do they actually operate by themselves like giant computers with no locatable will but with almost absolute power? Do they exist at all? Are they merely clusters of smaller entities? Do the smaller entities exist or submit to the the human will? Are we owned by the super-rich or are the super-rich themselves pawns of a monster they cannot control and which rules the world almost by accident? Is it a huge conspiracy, or an unnecessary accident? It is perhaps a measure of their power that it is possible to project onto Multi National Corporations any conspiracy theory without it seeming unlikely. Whatever the truth, they are a shadow stalking the common man, and impinging upon his everyday life which they control to varying undefinable degrees.

In this they resemble the bureaucratic giants such as the pre 1989 communist bloc states, and the EU.

Their gigantic controlling power leads us into paths we do not chose, and closes doors upon our attempts at self determination. They are a power that needs to be unravelled and resisted. To that end, and in preference to a giant conflagration it would almost certainly be a wise initial step to gradually lessen their power and size. The most easily perceived aspect of the Multi National Corporations is indeed their ever increasing size, and the way all profits in society actually seem to end up belonging to them. The money floats upwards towards where money already is, and it is increasingly difficult for any person or entity to make any profit by business. It is this effect which is just about still within the power of a democratically elected government to try to control and lessen and even to reverse. And that would be one of the fundamental tasks of a working class government. Not only in order to bring about the downwards flow of money in our economy for greater equality and for greater prosperity for all, but also to defend the very parliamentary democracy upon which our potential rights and hopes for self determination over our own destiny depends.

Capitalism, democracy and the freedom to make money

How could we protect small businesses?

A working class government should support the smaller players in the game of capitalism, dominated as it is by the very large players. If capitalism is supposed to be in any way connected to freedom, and democracy, then the drift towards the whole of the non-bureaucratic population becoming low paid employees of vast multinationals should be reversed.

A Working Class Alternative To Labour

Recently the Labour party has declared its intention to "be the party of small businesses". However, traditionally, Labour rank and file tends to regard the small businessman as a political opponent of the working classes, despite the fact that many working class people are self employed.

In fact, not only is the small businessman of primary importance in our economy, he represents the link between capitalism and democracy. The freedom capitalism is meant to give us, has to include the possibility for anyone/everyone to make money. When it becomes possible only for huge corporations to make money, then that freedom is in question; then it is time for a sort of revolution. Otherwise we will all become nothing but guests/ tenants/ wage-slaves in our society. When that happens, as it is happening now, our political rights, our rights as citizens, will shrink. This may happen imperceptibly, it may happen under cover of misleading jargon to make it seem as if our rights are expanding, but it will happen. Freedom is inexorably related to power. When citizens have no power then they have no freedom, and any rights they are granted are likely to be formulated to ensure that they operate more as fences to enclose them rather than real freedoms. National governments are not the only agencies to take away power and enclose the individual. Local governments are expert at taking powers unto themselves that national governments would think twice about - and getting away with it. Powerful corporations, banks and other private concerns, groups of powerful individuals, and highly organised interest groups, - these all aim to increase their power at the cost of the citizen or individual. The general trend in modern society is for large organisations, governmental or not, to increase their size and power, while the individual shrinks to powerless insignificance. Politics has to take this into account and people need to learn ways to reverse this process.

Governments are aware of the important economic role played by small businesses, even if that awareness stops short of helping them to survive in the *trickle-up* economy;
"Small businesses are a key part of the economy in terms of employment and growth. They account for around 50 per cent of UK business turnover, have more than 13 million employees, and pay more than a third of the tax receipts paid by businesses." (Her Majesty's Revenue and Customs).

Indeed, and without them there can be no recovery. And small businesses are not typically the ones paying minimum wages.

Policies should as often as possible tend towards moving money, and the making of profit in our society, downwards, instead of upwards. If the present *upwards* trend continues indefinately then it will eventually undermine the functioning of democracy. It is a notable feature of modern parties that they are not openly alert to this sort of danger when it is posed by elements *in the economy*. None of them relish the intellectual and political battle which has, at some time or other, to be fought against the power of multinationals. At the forefront of that battle is the small businessman, who is in the direct firing line of the larger concerns that sometimes even have deliberate strategies for putting him out of business.

A Working Class Alternative To Labour

At this stage of economic history, the polarisation of ownership has gone so far that there is now a natural alliance between the small or medium sized businessman and the low paid worker or the unemployed. All are being separated from the means of making money. The future prosperity of the country depends on both of them having a central rather than a peripheral role in the economy. That is why this collection of policies is not just a matter of getting justice for those currently low paid, but of making a new model for prosperity that can withstand the hard facts of the global economy. It means helping new businesses, especially in manufacturing.

One aim ought to be to make it possible for small businesses to compete in sectors where large concerns currently dominate.

One way to help small businesses would be to provide partial exemptions from the minimum wage, (see Agriculture below), and to create lower rates of pay for smaller businesses. A drawback is that it would make it difficult for these firms to compete in the labour market, the other of course is that even the smallest companies employ between them 7.5 million workers of whom maybe 60% are on wages lower than £9.30phr (although only 1 in 10 of their employees is on the current minimum wage). To make these employers exempt would leave 4 million people on less than £9.30phr. The solution then is to provide tax and business rates relief for smaller businesses instead, to cover their increase in labour costs. This would be worth more in money terms, and would help their overall ability to make profit and compete against larger firms.

New tax arrangements for businesses
Corporation Tax

This table shows how many of Britain's businesses are micro, small and medium (SMEs=Small and medium Enterprises), and what share of the national turnover they take, and what proportion of the workforce they employ ("No employees" refers to sole traders and partnerships which have no employees).

	Number of enterprises	Employment	Turnover billions
Micro 0-9	4, 580 000	7, 750,000	624
(of which No employees)	3, 557 000	3, 902,000	208)
Small 10-49	178, 000	3,471, 000	454
Medium 50-249	30 000	2,909000	450
TOTAL SMEs	4, 788 000	14 ,130, 000	1 529
Large 250+	6 000	9, 763, 000	1 603
Total, all Enterprises	4, 794 000	23, 893 000	3 132
SMEs as % of total	99.00%	59.00%	49.00%
Micro as % of total	96.00%	32.00%	20.00%

(Source: House of Commons)

As you can see, 99% of businesses are micro, small or medium sized, and these make up 49% of the turnover, and account for 59% of all employment. They also account for one third of all the corporation tax paid to the Treasury *(Source: HMRC).*

Small companies profit margins are often narrower than larger businesses. This tends to be reflected to some degree in the amount of tax businesses end up paying. But as you can see below, the present tax bands aren't always sufficient to make much difference. Economies of scale still mean that smaller businesses make less profit and cant compete with larger ones. In a competitive market this contributes to the overall trend of trickle-up, where the huge companies get bigger and richer, and the rest of us are left struggling. If we say the smaller businesses taken as a whole, make on average 6% profit on their turnover and the larger ones make on average 10%, then we can see how there is a need for a significant banding in the taxation.

Businesses making profit of 6% on turnover	Businesses making profit of 10% on turnover
do £1000 of business	do £1000 of business
make £60 profit	make £100profit
pay £12 tax (20%)	pay £23 tax (23%)
left with £48	left with £77

To even this up somewhat, so that the first group of businesses would be left with £60 and the second with £65, you could remove all the first group, typically small businesses, from tax, and put the rate up for the second group, typically large businesses, to 35%. This incidentally is still less than the highest band rate in the USA (a country we think of as having low tax). If we stopped far short of that,

33

and made instead top rates of 26% and 27% (leaving our example company with roughly £74) just above what it was in 2011, then you could still afford to reduce the first group's tax to 15% (leaving them £51).

Here is a list of the G20 nations and their Corporation Taxes, for comparison:

UK 20- 23%

USA 15 - 39%

France 33%

Germany 29%

Japan 38%

Russia 20%/6% for small businesses

China 25%

Brazil 35%

India 30%

Turkey 20%

Austrailia 30%

Italy 31%

Austria 25%

Belgium 33%

Canada 15%

Czech Republic 19%

Denmark 25%

Finland 24%

Ireland 25/12/10%

Netherlands 25%

Norway 28%

Spain 30/24%

Sweden 22%

A Working Class Alternative To Labour

The USA has the highest nominal rate in the G20 nations, but that it is banded (in fact there are 4 bands between $0 and $335,000 profits); but roughly speaking, companies earning up to $50,000 pay 15%, while companies earning over $335,000 pay 39% up to $10m after which they pay 35%.

In Britain at present there are only 2 rates;

Profit	tax
up to £300,000	20%
£300,000 +	23%

There is hardly any difference between the rates and certainly not enough to help companies with lower profits. So, to help small and medium businesses, and to reverse the trickle-up effect, Corporation Tax in Britain could be banded, like Income Tax. This would require a higher top rate to make up for it, a slightly bigger contribution from the wealthiest companies, but still nothing like the 39% they are asked to pay in the USA.

It could be something like this:

Profit	tax
0 - £10,000	0%
£10,000 - £20,000	7%
£20,000 - £30,000	10%
£30,000 - £150,000	15%
£150,000 - £300,000	20%
£300,000 - £3m	26%
£3m +	27%

This is a spreading of the tax burden upwards; the income to the Treasury would be roughly the same as now, whilst giving small businesses a significant easing from tax to offset the added labour costs from the higher minimum wage. Many businesses are already not paying low wages, of course, and so would benefit all the more. The zero rating for businesses until they are making £10,000 clear profit would help many struggling shops and businesses to survive, as would the relief from the burdensome business rates which would be replaced with a banded tax (see below).

Abolish Business Rates (called Non-domestic Rates) and replace it with a banded Local Business Tax.

Government raises £24bn in Business Rates (Non-domestic Rates), and it is intended as income for local government to pay for services. It is raised by a yearly tax paid on the value of premises. The Business Rates have grown to be an almost insupportable burden to the small shopkeeper who is now often paying more in rates than in rent for his business premises. Many shops close merely because of Business Rates. It would be beneficial to our economy, if we intend to move the power to make money downwards, to shift some more of the burden for the £24bn onto the shops and businesses with the highest turnovers. We could abolish the Business Rates and replace them with a new business tax, a banded tax, similar to Income Tax, and based on *turnover* shown in the tax accounts already supplied to HMRC. At present there are 1.7 million businesses premises paying the Business Rates. The bottom 1.2 million businesses (that's 70% of the total) pay between them only £1.7bn out of the total of

£24bn. To remove the need for them to pay Business Rates altogether would only require that the top 30% of businesses get a 7% rise in their rates bill. In other words a large store paying £44,000 now would pay £47,000. The result of this slight adjustment would be that more than one million shops and small businesses would be helped to survive. The high streets in particular would receive a boost that would reverse the pattern of shop closures that have blighted them.

Basing the payments on existing accounts would prevent extra paper work for businesses, and would make collection cheaper. It would also obviate the expensive revaluations by the Valuation Office.

Basing a new Local Business Tax on turnover would also mean that in times of a downturn in business the tax would be lower. The present Non-domestic Rates stay the same no matter how bad business is, which is forcing many shops to close; they even levy Non-domestic Rates on empty shops, which has led some landlords to knock premises down rather than pay the rates.

(While commercial office premises could be taxed in the new way, non-commercial office rentals would have to be charged according to the Non-domestic Rates system as now).

Small and medium businesses and the Minimum wage of £9.30phr.

There are roughly 4.5m micro/small businesses, employing 7.7m people.

According to the Federation of Small Businesses, which surveyed its members, asking questions about the Living Wage (£7.45, £8.30 in London), the average size of firm is 10 employees. Of those 6 are on more than the Living Wage, 1.2 is on the Living Wage, 2.1 are on between the £6.30 and £7.45 (£8.30 in London), and 1 is on the minimum wage.

According to a study *(Beyond the bottom line, Matthew Pennycook and Kayte Lawton)* the average labour costs increase for small businesses caused by the Living Wage of £7.45 (£8.30 in London) would be, varying from sector to sector, between 1% and 6%. This included the phenomenon of *spill*, which means that people on higher wages expect to get rises to keep their differentials. Remember that is the cost of a rise from £6.30 to £7.45, which is 18%. This book is suggesting a bigger rise, of 32%. The costs to small businesses could be said to be around double those predicted for the Living Wage, so between 2% and 12%. This can be seen in the light of the proposed abolition of Business Rates for most small businesses, and the substantial reduction in Corporation Tax. These taxes normally represent about a third of *overall* costs (33%), and their removal would more than compensate for the increase in labour costs (12% of *only labour* costs).

A Prices and Wages Commission

To prevent the proposed wage rises being clawed back by industry as price rises, (which is what happened in the 1960s and 70s) there would have to be a prices commission powerful enough to impose fines on firms making inflationary price rises. This system is used very successfully in Austria for example. (Austria has one of the best records on the eradication of poverty in Europe). Essentially the rise in wages for the low paid would be a social and economic revolution, and a working class government would have to take firm action on prices to uphold the claim on profits, otherwise it would not happen. And it would be a new relative status amongst wage earners which would have to be defended. For this reason, the recent (*UK Citizens*) campaign for a living wage would need the support of a sympathetic government to prevent it resulting merely in inflation. It is hard to imagine the present middle class Labour party having the will to give that support, even if only by making the Living Wage compulsory.

Rent caps

To stop the higher minimum wage being passed on as inflation, it is not just prices that have to be regulated but rents also. If this were not done landlords, including those who own retail premises, might be tempted to try to take back money by simply putting up rents. For this reason there could be a cap of around 3% per year for rent increases.

This would have two effects; one would be to prevent inflation linked to the new minimum wage, but it would also serve to build in a steady and controlled growth in the rental market, and help prevent the property value explosion that was the ruin of the global economy. Along with other measures described here, it would build an idea of an acceptable level of profit in our society (a radical idea which could be eventually expanded to govern all trade and growth). It would allow for steady economic growth across the board, rather than growth in the value of property, and growth of existing wealth. In other words, it would mean that growth would have to come from manufactures that add things to the nation's wealth, rather than from writing bigger and bigger price tags above existing buildings, and calling that "value". That process adds nothing to most people's real wealth, it merely results in us all paying what is in effect vast rents to the banks for property we think we own. It makes the banks richer, and everyone else poorer.

Rent control of retail outlets would revolutionise the situation for small retailers, They are often bled for high rents by property owners, which is one of the reasons why high street shops are dying. This phenomenon is typical of the way money in our society drifts upwards, towards the banks or large owners, so that it is difficult for anyone else to make a living.

This control of rents would be a vital part of a working class government's policies aimed at moving money **downwards** in the economy and preventing the polarising effects we have seen in recent decades.

In recent months, Labour has belatedly responded to the Living Wage Campaign by talking about voluntary agreements by employers (maybe hoping to get credit for higher wages without doing anything to bring them about).But it's hard to see where they expect a higher minimum wage to lead to without such measures as *price control* and *rent control*, except to inflation. It could look as if they fully expect inflation driven by capital, and accept it. The working classes need a party that is strongly and openly committed to getting for them a larger slice of the pie and defending that position.

It says something about the Labour Party, whose purpose it is supposed to be to represent the interests of the working classes, that they had to get the idea of even a limited increase in wages from the *UK Citizens* organisation. It ought to be an obvious move for them, especially after the demise of the unions. How else do they expect the lives of the working classes they represent to improve? By benefits handouts, family tax credits, or maybe unemployment benefit? The state of the economy leaves them no room for manoeuvre, as government is still over-spending by £120bn even under the Conservatives. There is simply no money to spend in handouts, and all they can do is offer to borrow it. The last time Labour despaired of waiting for a surplus and borrowed in order to alleviate poverty, in 2002, is when the current government deficit began.

Given all that, the *only* way to alleviate poverty in Britain is through higher wages (any net increase in unemployment related payments can only be made if government tax receipts increase as a result of higher wages). Presumably Labour realise this, and intend to simply avoid mentioning to the electorate that they will have to borrow more money and go further into debt, or do nothing about poverty.

The Agriculture Sector - Another example of the Trickle Up economy.

There are 200,000 low paid jobs in agriculture. Who benefits from the fact that agricultural labourers are paid very low wages? Is it the farmers? If so, is it small farmers or large farming conglomerates? Or is it the retailers with the power to control the prices farmers can get for their produce because of their huge, almost exclusive, purchasing power?

In fact farming is just another sector where the large corporations have the upper hand and benefit from the low labour costs in that industry. Agriculture is not labour intensive; only 1.5% of the workforce are in agriculture, producing 60% of what we eat; the rest is imported.

Small farmers are unable to make ends meet because of the big stores pushing the prices of their produce down.

Of the 400,000 people working in agriculture, 200,000 are on low wages. The profit from their labour goes not to the small farmers (because they are not making any significant profits) but to the large conglomerates who own the land, or to supermarkets who make profits on the sale.

Because the balance in agriculture has gone so far in favour of the large owners already it would be appropriate to give small farmers a partial exemption from the minimum wage of £9.30, to provide a lever in their favour in competition with the larger concerns. The rate might be something like £8.00, and it should be based on turnover. (They can't be helped through tax relief as they are exempt from Business Rates already, and make too little profit to pay much tax).

A price commission should protect small farmers from the buying power of the big retailers, to stop the *downwards* pressure on prices.

Farmers, unlike other producers, should be entitled to pass on the wage rises to their customers, who are mainly the large stores.

So, the large employers would have higher labour costs while the smaller farms would benefit from their increased price competitiveness due to lower labour costs.

Higher wages would push up the cost of food to the supermarkets who would pass on that cost to the consumer (they would be entitled to do this as they would be passing on material costs not labour costs. If supermarkets put up prices beyond what was due to actual increases in commodity prices they would be liable to fines, See *Prices and Wages Commission*, above). This would mean inflation in food prices. However, the low labour intensity of the agriculture industry would mean that price rises would be marginal. Labour costs represent roughly 10% of production costs, so an increase in labour costs brought about by the minimum wage being raised from £6 to £9, i.e. 50%, would be a 50% rise in 10% of the cost, i.e. a net rise of 5%. Food prices would go up by 5%. The working classes' pay would have been increased by 50%, and so they would still have 45% more purchasing power than now. The middle classes who spend a smaller proportion of their total expenditure on food, would notice the 5% in food prices increase even less.

Land Ownership

It is also worth noting that land ownership is following the same pattern as ownership of everything else; the ordinary person, in this case the farmer, is being forced out by the big businesses.

Across the whole of Europe 50% of land is owned by 3% of farms *(Source:Transnational Institute)*. And widespread buying up of land by conglomerates is forcing ordinary people off the land. In Britain it is estimated that 70% of the land is owned by 1% of the population (*Source: UK Land Directory*).

The trend is *world wide*, as China and Russia and the west land-grab in Africa, *Europe wide* as the conglomerates do the same here, and *Britain wide* as Britain has a high degree of land ownership concentration.

Here is an extract of a report given to the European parliament:

"Across Europe...changes are being driven by agricultural policies, national and European, that benefit large agribusiness and are causing severe economic, social and cultural marginalization of small and medium scale farmers.

"At the European level, the CAP (the EU Common Agricultural Policy) - which is the vehicle for delivering the European Community's vision for agriculture – does nothing to support the development of small-scale agriculture despite clear evidence that it is the form of agriculture most beneficial for our environment and communities.

"The numerous impacts are visible in the whole of Europe. It leads to the closing down of hundreds of farms each year which are replaced by highly mechanized agribusiness operating on an industrial model, resulting in a widespread reduction in rural employment.

A Working Class Alternative To Labour

"These issues are increasing rural to urban migration and the corresponding growth of cities. All over Europe, land grabbing and industrial farming are maintaining a similar pace as human migrations and the exploitation of workers, very often farmers expelled from their lands. Thousands of people travel huge distances to work as a cheap and flexible labour force in poor conditions with low wages in European agro-industrial companies.

"Land grabbing and land concentration go hand in hand with the industrialization of food production lines and the standardization of food products. European citizens have become dependent on the vagaries of large retailers."

(Report by *European Coordination Via Campesina* presented to the European Parliament in 2013).

The most telling point in the report is that the large scale mechanisation of agriculture was bad for the consumer, in terms of the quality of the food, as well as for farmers, communities and the environment. It suits only the large producers.

Hopefully the small wages advantage, plus to a lesser degree the beneficial new tax arrangements for all small businesses, would tip the balance slightly towards the smaller farmer. The recovery of small local shops would also benefit them, as systems of local production and delivery would recover in the long run.

A Return to Manufacturing

Our balance of payments is in deficit (£4bn per month, the second largest monthly deficit in the world). We buy more than we sell. Germany and Denmark and Holland and Sweden, for example, are in credit. If we don't ourselves make more of what we use, it can only get worse. For Britain to be able to pay its way in the future we need a return to manufacturing.

Much of British industry (except, for example, aerospace and weapons, which still flourish), was pushed into decline during the 1980s at great cost to the country, which now depends largely on financial services (investment banking) for its balance of payments. This means that we **export money**, we invest in foreign industry. One third of all profits invested is now invested abroad. A short term solution holding the seeds of long term disaster. It has already left a whole class permanently redundant and has given us a built-in imbalance of wages distribution. It does this by removing money from manufacture in Britain, creating unemployment, and creating very lucrative jobs for the relatively few people involved in investment banking. It will only get worse as foreign industries grow and ours shrink even further. Obviously it makes Britain extra vulnerable to financial crises, as we have recently learned to our great cost. A conclusive banking collapse would spell disaster for a country that relies, not on manufacture, but on investment banking for its balance of payments. We need to go back into production and export so we can pay for the huge number of imported goods we buy each year.

Because of the low wage message that has been drummed into us over 3 decades, since the dramatic decline of much of British industry under the Tories, we tend to think that it is impossible to manufacture our own goods because the economies of the far east do it cheaper. This obviously hasn't occurred to the Germans, or even the Danes or Swedes with their high wages, for they all have a balance of payments surplus despite not relying on high finance for a large part of their income as we do. The high paid Danes and Swedes, whose working classes have long since kissed goodbye to the kind of poverty ours expect, and who enjoy high standards of living, export more than they import; both they and the Germans hold their own (and not only in high quality engineering), while we have largely given up due to poor investment and poor education.

We have taken the view that if it is made cheaper elsewhere it makes no sense to make it here. British politicians talk of relying on British "expertise" and high value exports as if the Chinese don't have expertise of their own and rely on us to tell them how to build bridges. That is nonsense (the idea is based on the fact that one of our main service sector exports is engineering consultancy), and the Chinese and other nations are simply overtaking us in *all* areas, including education, while we are well on the way to becoming a third rate nation, relying on foreign manufacture for the *whole range* of products that we use.

The hard truth is, if we can't afford to make it then in the long term we can't afford to use it.

Isn't there a contradiction between the ideas of greater investment and higher wages?

It might seem that high minimum wage policies that effectively remove one third of owners' profits and give them out in wages contradicts the idea of greater investment in British industry, because the money to invest comes from the profits of industry.

However, since 1980s and the decline of British manufacturing, the rate of internal investment has declined. Now fully one third of profits are invested abroad (£68bn invested abroad by UK companies in 2011). In other words, big business and high finance is not doing the job of investing in British industry. Higher wages would mean taking away some of the profits from big business and high finance; But it would make it possible for small account holders to save, and those savings are what traditional banking used to use to fund local businesses (see **Small High Street Savings Banks**, below).

What is the meaning of imports when we have 3 million unemployed?

Unemployment is the direct consequence of under-investment in industry

Twenty-one per cent of 16-24 yr olds are unemployed, 460,000 are seeking Job Seeker's Allowance.

Overall, there are 900,000 people who have been unemployed longer than one year *(Source: Department of Works and Pensions)*.

Long term unemployment is a social problem and an economic one. The social costs of young people being in long term unemployment go towards making our society destructive and negative. The economic costs include housing benefit, and unemployment benefit and other social security payments, also social services, prison services and other attendant costs of long term unemployment. The other cost is wasted labour; wasted labour that costs money to feed and house. Wasted labour that suffers a massive disappointment and disillusionment at the beginning of its working life, a sense of being not needed, and not wanted.

This is because we have chosen to live the lie that we can somehow pay for what we use by high finance investing in foreign industry instead of our own young people's lives.

It is a disgraceful waste of young people's hopes and potential, a destructive and negative choice, that young working class people correctly interpret as an expression of contempt towards them. This is what gives rise to the impression that the poor are a burden upon the rich, whereas the opposite is the truth, as it is the rich who are a burden upon the poor, for it is the rich who live upon the profits produced by anyone who is paid less than the profit they generate by their work.

In fact it is the unemployed, and perhaps especially the young unemployed, who are the key to our future recovery. They are the unused manpower that can increase our collective wealth and prosperity. Theirs are the hands that can manufacture the commodities that we need so that we don't need to buy them from abroad.

How did it ever happen that we decided that it was better for those in work to support 3 million out of work, so that we can buy foreign goods instead of making them ourselves? How did anyone think that the "cheap" foreign goods were still cheap when to their price was added the cost of paying for the unemployed?

Although the decline of British manufacturing began long before 1979, the Thatcher government's monetarist policies dealt some final blows. *"In the early 1980s net investment was negative, not enough to maintain existing stock... and by 1983 output was at the same levels as it had been during the 3 day week, and imports in manufactured goods exceeded exports for the first time since the beginning of the Industrial Revolution. By 1985, 2.5 million jobs had been lost in manufacturing since 1970, and half of those had been lost between 1979 and 1985."* (Peter Donaldson, A Question of Economics 1985).

The high interest rates, inflated pound and low investment made it impossible for many industries to compete with the cheap imports those policies made possible, and many went finally to the wall, never to return. But problems in management and unions, workforce and investment, training and education, that had hampered Britain since the war, were perhaps not very different from the ones that are preventing our recovery now.

A Working Class Alternative To Labour

The hard-nosed, level-headed, business minded Tories, who were so enamoured of the notion of a quick buck to be made by the city, failed in their calculations. They imagined that workers from failed manufacturing would get new jobs in the service industries in a shiny new Britain where a "modernised" workforce would magically balance the trade figures, not by making and selling, but by doing services to one another. Oddly they never thought how we would *pay* for ourselves to provide services for one another. It would have worked if we no longer bought and used commodities, and only provided services ranging from health care to filing each others' nails.

But since we *do* buy commodities, the policy of closing British industries down and making ourselves unemployed has sent this country into long term decline that cannot be reversed until we go back to making what we use. We hid the illogicality of the situation from ourselves until the banks crashed and the balloon burst. Then it was shown that Britain was particularly vulnerable to a banking crisis, and that we have too weak a manufacturing base to be able to expect a speedy recovery. The governments look in vain for green shoots where things haven't grown for decades because things haven't been planted.

Other countries, again the high-wage/low-poverty economies of Northern Europe, were only marginally affected by the global recession.
Meanwhile the British government has a debt of £1200bn, the 4th largest by amount in the world.

51

What is the National Debt?

It is the amount of money the government owes to the private sector. At present it stands at around £1200bn. That is about 75% of the GDP (GDP=what we produce per year).

Who owns the debt?
In the past it was usually held internally, now a third of it is held by foreign banks.
The Bank of England owns 25% of it.
Other banks and building societies own 10% of it.
Pension funds and insurance companies own 25% of it.
Foreign holdings own 30% of it.
Others, including households, 10%

What is it?
It is more correctly called the Public Sector Net Debt because it is the result of accumulated yearly borrowing by the government to meet its annual spending requirements. Government spending, (NHS, defence, social security etc.) at present exceeds what the government gets in from taxation.

Is the debt decreasing or increasing?
The debt is increasing because the government is still spending more than it gets in taxes, by about £120bn per year. (Recently the monthly figures indicated it was around £116bn). That is about 8% of the GDP (just after the crash it went up to 11%). Government spending has gone down only slightly, but it now represents a smaller *proportion* of the GDP as revenues have increased.

Is that level of debt high?
The debt is higher now than it was in 2002, and higher than it was in 1991. If you judge the debt by how big a percentage of the GDP it represents, then in those years it was lower than it had been since 1912. Between 1916 and 1952 the debt was more than 150% of the GDP.

So if it is lower than it has been for a lot of the century, why does it matter?
It is harder for the UK to borrow at good rates than it was then. In 1952 Britain received a large loan from the USA (to pay for the cost of fighting the war against Nazi Germany, which we have only just paid off). That is not likely now, as America too is in debt. The global crash means that it is harder to borrow, especially for the UK which has a higher debt to GDP ratio than many other countries, and the 4th largest debt by amount in the world. Everyone, including the private sector, is in debt and so there is less saving, and so the government cannot sell its bonds (IOUs with interest) as easily (another disadvantage of keeping one third of the population in poverty is that they can't buy government bonds).

Interest rates might go up suddenly and that would have a disastrous affect on the government's ability to spend. Repayments now cost £48bn per year, half as much as the NHS.

It matters also because the government is already having to borrow to meet its spending; if interest rates went up we would get rapidly deeper into debt.

Just as with a household's debt, even a large debt might not matter if you are earning enough to pay the interest, and if you don't have to keep borrowing. But if your income *doesn't* cover your debt repayments and interest, and you have to *borrow to pay even the interest on your debt*, then you are in trouble. And that is our position, as the government is borrowing £120bn per year, 2.7 times what the debt repayments are.

Why did the debt suddenly get so big since 2002?

Partly because of the Labour government's high levels of spending on the NHS and on social security (including in-work benefits). After 2008 and the crash, tax receipts fell drastically, because the economy shrank and because the receipts from stamp duty (tax on house sales) fell dramatically. So the government had to borrow more to fill the gap in its finances.

Does the National debt have anything to do with the trade deficit?

Not directly. Another measurement, the <u>Net International Investment Position</u>, shows a more complete picture; it shows the net of the country's external liabilities and assets, it includes both government *and* private external debt. Britain's position is a net *liability* of -£182bn 2012 *(Source: Office of National Statistics)*. Germany's position is net *assets* of + £776bn *(Source: Eurostat)*.

This comparison with Germany can be seen along with that of the UK and Germany's trade figures, where Germany has an annual trade *surplus* of £136bn and the UK has a *deficit* of £43bn. Germany is at the top of the international tables for trade, second is China, the UK is fourth from last.

So when we talk of the impossibility of competing with the eastern countries with their cheap labour, we can remember that Germany which has higher wages than we do, does more than compete, they lead the world.

And it is Germany, not China, we import most from. And if you look at the list of goods that Germany produces, and what we import from them, there is nothing we shouldn't be able to produce ourselves. While if you look at our top exports... in 14 of our top 20 exports we are net importers anyway. *(Source: H.M. Customs and Excise)*.

And in case you are thinking it's just those Germans who are so efficient who manage to compete and produce a trade surplus, look at Denmark, the Netherlands and Sweden. All countries with high wages; in Denmark they have an average wage of £600, where ours is £346. They don't have poverty like we do, and despite being a small country with no huge natural resources, they pay their way, they have a trade surplus.

We have every reason to be ashamed. Looking at the figures, the resources and the potential, our abject position in just about every table seems to be the result of sheer stupidity and mismanagement, the wrong decisions. There is no point blaming one party or one group of people, we are all to blame. But it's time we changed course.

Do we have to pay off the national debt - What's the point of austerity measures?

British governments, along with many other governments, have spent more than they get in from taxes. Each year they face a shortfall of around £120bn. They can do a few things, or a combinations of things; they can cut spending to within what they can afford, or they can increase taxes to raise money, or they can borrow the money to spend what they want to spend. Or they can cut spending by a little bit and borrow the rest. The present government is doing the latter.

The shortfall is so vast that it is hard to make any inroads on it by cuts. Government spending, such as social security spending, usually benefits the less well off, and to cut that spending causes hardship which any government wants to avoid. If they raise taxes, it is unpopular at the ballot box, because most people resent taxation (although they expect the services it pays for) and most people in Britain think we pay more tax than other countries even though we pay less than many comparable European countries; it's just something people insist on believing.

The list below shows the overall tax burden of each country in Europe as a percentage of GDP. This is not just income tax, but includes National Insurance, sales taxes (VAT), Corporation Tax, Council Tax. *(Source: Eurostat).*

Austria 42%
Belgium 44%
Britain 36%
Bulgaria 27%
Czech Republic 34%

Denmark 47%

Finland 43%

France 44%

Germany 39%

Hungary 37%

Ireland 29%

Italy 42%

Luxembourg 37%

Netherlands 39%

Norway 42%

Poland 32%

Portugal 33%

Romania 28%

Spain 31%

Sweden 43%

Governments that put up tax always have it used against them by other parties at elections, even though those other parties may be planning tax hikes themselves. Governments try to hide taxes from the people for this reason. In fact it would be quite a good way of raising money for spending and, in fact, it's the most logical and the fairest way, since a society ought to expect to pay for what it spends. Also, a progressive tax system, such as ours in Britain, generally works in such a way as to put the burden mainly upon the better off (no matter what party political propagandists try to say about their opponents' taxation ideas in particular), and that is another reason why Income Tax, which is banded, is a relatively fair way of raising money to cover a shortfall in the government finances (Corporation Tax, which is hardly banded, isn't). Apart from unpopularity, another problem with tax is that it can stifle an economy. Mainly though, the problem with it is that there is little scope for Income Tax increases before a government finds itself voted out by the electorate. People are sufficiently illogical to blame a government for debt, budget deficit *and* high tax. It is not uncommon to hear someone complaining about too much tax, *and* demanding more and better services in the same breath.

A look at the British Parliament website will reveal the kind of amounts that can be raised by putting up certain taxes; A penny each on Income Tax, National Insurance, VAT and Corporation Tax, could raise about £10bn. To get any more than that would require more drastic measures such as removing current VAT exemptions (on food), abolishing first-residence capital gains exemptions, and abolishing the lower Corporations Tax rate for small companies (the suggestion in this book is to raise the higher rate for big companies). Most of that would directly affect the incomes of the low paid, and would therefore be politically hard to do. But it would raise another £35bn. Remember the spending shortfall is £120bn. You can see how hard it is for governments to balance their books. Because of the recession, receipts from taxes went down by roughly £40bn per year (this does mean that even without the recession, the shortfall would still be £80bn each year). It is clear from this that business is bad, we are not paying our way.

How did government spending get to be so much more than tax receipts?

Between 1979 and 1987 the budget deficit was around £10bn, kept low despite high unemployment benefit spending, by the North Sea gas revenues. The budget even showed a surplus in 1988 and 1989 under Major's chancellorship. Then, under Lamont, the Exchange Rate Mechanism and Black Wednesday disasters, and a recession, shrank tax receipts and so pushed up borrowing, which rose to £50bn. A recovery plus some spending cuts under Ken Clark reduced the yearly deficit, from £50bn to £15bn, and that course was held by Gordon Brown who was able, as the economy expanded under Labour, to show a surplus for 4 years until 2002, when increased spending on NHS and social security to reduce poverty, resulted in a return to deficit, which grew to £40bn. When the banking crisis hit and the recession followed, the deficit leapt up to a staggering £156bn, as tax receipts fell drastically and unemployment benefits spending rose sharply.

And don't forget the debt itself, the accumulation of each year's deficit; this reached £1200bn. More than a trillion. (The USA debt meanwhile has reached such apocalyptic proportions that American commentators are now saying it will never be paid. Perhaps they shouldn't say that too loudly in case their creditors hear and it starts another global recession. Such a position does in fact put the long term future of the USA in doubt).

While the deficit comes from a variety of causes, the biggest increases have been caused by external events, if recession can be called that. What is clear though is that not balancing the budget, spending more than we can afford, at least puts the government's yearly finances in a vulnerable position.

And once such a huge debt has been created, it is very difficult to get rid of it without severe cuts in spending and the accompanying hardship, as well as rises in taxation. This is largely because the same factors which contributed to it continue to add to it, and the scope for cuts is small compared to the size of the debt.

As anyone who has been in serious debt knows, recovery from that position cannot begin while you are still spending more than you get in, because then the debt is growing, while the interest on the debt is one of the factors pushing you further into debt. The government is having to pay £48bn (equivalent to half the NHS budget) per year on debt repayments.

Those who think you don't have to worry about national debt believe that debt is alright if you can pay the interest, and carry on. And that is true up to a point. But we *cannot* pay the interest. We are *borrowing* further to pay it. And the worse your finances are the harder it is to get loans on good terms. That is a debt spiral, and it can only end in disaster.

That disaster would be: an eventual inability to borrow further without very severe cuts being imposed as a condition, (such as those imposed upon Greece); a drop in living standards; a shrinking of the economy; unemployment, and further cuts in spending. It would mean more poverty for the already poor, and a collapse of public services, including the NHS and social security.

As things stand, there is no very convincing plan for addressing the debt. The Chancellor has recently reduced the yearly deficit from £120bn to £116bn, (based on monthly figures), but we are then still £116bn off being able to reduce the debt. The government is still spending more than it gets in. And before it spends anything it has to spend £48bn on the debt interest.

But this much is clear, even if we don't plan to pay off the debt or even reduce it in the near future, spending over the budget requires new loans, and the need to get new loans makes that spending vulnerable.

For this reason, either spending has to go down, if it is wasteful, or new sources of income for government are needed, to supply that shortfall.

Another ten years of this and the National Debt will double.

Balancing the budget and starting to pay off the debt

The suggestions in this book identify both *areas for cuts in spending*, as well as ways of *increasing the government's revenue*. These have already been outlined. They are: 1. The cuts to in-work benefits (which are at present at £60bn and could be substantially reduced) that would come from a high minimum wage 2. The increase to government tax revenues which the high minimum wage would bring, through Income Tax and National Insurance receipts. The higher spending would also increase VAT revenue (on the money being spent by workers, one third of which money would otherwise be leaving the country as outward investment).

If there was an accompanying use of the new savings of higher paid workers, as investment for small businesses, then unemployment would reduce and those in new work would also be paying income tax where they were absorbing it before in benefits.

Competitiveness of British Industry with a high minimum wage

Foreign businesses are not at present necessarily attracted to low wage Britain, as the past 50 years have shown. Problems of low productivity compared to say the higher paid German workers, have made Britain less attractive to companies, British or foreign (it seems strange to talk of attracting foreign companies when we neglect the need to have more of our own). Higher wages would address that very problem. The cheapskate British method has not proved successful, as a demoralised, underpaid workforce is unlikely to be as committed to a company's success as one that is paid well. Co-operation in industry is part of success. Remuneration and training are both a part of this.

The passive mode of trying to attract foreign businesses to Britain by making ourselves cheap, was only ever likely to lead to long term decline, as even when it works it creates a haemorrhage of money from the country and pushes British firms further out of the field. We need a well-paid and well-educated workforce who have the associated high productivity rates (as opposed to a low paid and partially illiterate and innumerate one) for our own industries, to create a strong domestic market as a launch pad for exports. Or we need high paying foreign companies who want skilled labour. The very last thing we need is to attract low paying foreign companies, who *import* components for an unskilled workforce to assemble.

All of the measures which take money from corporations and put it back into the economy through wages contribute to the reduction of investment in foreign companies, and to the availability of funds for investment in our own. The revolution in wages, which will leave working class families with a monthly surplus, could be combined with a new type of high street local lending bank,which would put their savings to work as investment in small businesses (see "banking" below).

Foreign Companies in Low Wage Britain

For decades, desperate to see new jobs created as British manufacturing declined, governments have talked about attracting foreign firms to Britain. But it is not a good long-term solution to unemployment if the workforce is insufficiently skilled and is therefore low paid. The foreign-owned businesses are likely in that case to be nothing more then assembly plants.

Mass production of cars for example, doesn't just require one big factory, there has to be a large network of engineering works with skilled workers to make tools and components. When that network is gone, as it is in Britain, then the high value work is done elsewhere and all we do is to assemble the parts. Remember too that in an assembly plant, where the parts that are assembled are brought in from abroad, they are counted as imports. So a £10,000 car assembled here brings very little value into the British economy, in fact it takes it out. The £10,000 goes to the owner, say Fiat, and the £5000 or so imported parts count as a deficit on our current account. The only benefit of each car assembled here is the low wages paid to the assembly plant operatives, and the tax on the profits which is paid at one of the lowest in Europe, 23%. (see table p.33)

Britain needs to develop that support structure of skilled engineering works that would make it possible to properly manufacture, for example cars, here in Britain. That means investment, training and education. It means ensuring that school leavers are literate and numerate and able to train as skilled engineering workers. At present it is doubtful that we have sufficient numbers of school or college leavers of a high enough proficiency in practical engineering to enable us to have a car manufacturing industry here. So we import cars, or assemble them. Meanwhile governments talk of British exports being 'high value, highly skilled engineering'. This is because the exports we do have are typically of that nature, such as in aerospace and arms manufacture. But those claims tend to gloss over the fact that we lack the ability to manufacture the majority of what we use.

A productive economy where skilled workers received high wages would not of course put off foreign companies. Foreign companies would be attracted to the stronger domestic market for goods, created by a higher wage economy. A low-wage, low-affluence economy has limited potential as a market for high-value goods. What manufacturer, foreign or British, would be excited by the prospect of locating its high-value manufacture in a country whose high streets are filled with pound shops, a country with weak retail sales based on low incomes? It is prosperity that is attractive and propitious to business, not poverty.

To drive down wages is to unnecessarily shrink the economy. In an economy based on consumption prosperity has to be based on manufacturing. There are two things we need to do to pay our way - one is to produce for export, the other is to produce more of what we use ourselves so we don't have to buy it from abroad; this would leave money for fuel for example, some of which we *have* to buy from abroad (until we re-open the pits to extract the coal that lies beneath British soil; world reserves are 860bn tonnes and we have about 3bn of them. We produce only 30% of the coal we use, and coal provides 38.4% of our energy. That's a lot of imported energy).

Don't we need to compete with cheap foreign labour?

When we produce what we use ourselves, (not for export) we *don't have to* compete with foreign prices, and their cheap labour (and cheap means something like 5% of western labour costs). Each time you buy a cheap foreign item you are contributing to our poverty because the money leaves the country, and because it contributes to the trade deficit, and because it means that we are idle and without work, while we need or use more things than ever. It has to be paid for, so does unemployment benefit.

The advantage to the consumer of a low wage, low quality product is an illusion created by not taking quality and durability into account. Many foreign producers are not producing the same product cheaper, they are producing a poorer product cheaply. For years we have been closing down our own production and, as consumers, accepting poorer products. The housewife who buys a cheap toaster despite knowing that it will likely break within a short time, is putting her own husband out of work, unfairly (if there was not a quality difference it wouldn't be unfair, it would just be unwise). By lowering our standards for products we have effectively been giving long term loans to foreign producers so that one day they will be able to produce products of a better quality. That subsidy to foreign producers has been at the expense of our own, which it has helped put out of business; it has taught us to say of ourselves that we can't compete with foreign, cheap, low wage producers.

The Cheap Foreign Toaster, a cheap and cheerful look at one.

Toaster price	£5.00
replacement after 2 years	£5.00
again after 4 years	£5.00

again after 6 years	£5.00
again after 8 years	£5.00
subtotal	£25.00
indirect costs	unemployment
	unemployment benefit
	social services/prison
	trade deficit
	falling wages
	falling tax receipts
	government debt
	govt borrowing
	spending cuts/poverty
	even lower wages
Total price	national decline

The "cheap toaster" The cost of the cheap toaster is not £5 it is more like £25 (even without including the cost of unemployment). If a British manufacturer produces a toaster for £25 (providing he makes it well and that we have the support industries to make the components), the consumer needs to be induced to include durability in her calculations.

Perhaps giving long guarantees would be a simple way. And if we do produce our own commodities then the benefits will be two-fold; a better balance of payments, and an end to high unemployment.

But, why not just buy it where it is made cheaply?

A cheap toaster costs a remarkable £5. It is made ..abroad, where labour is cheap, but getting less cheap.

We think we can't make it as cheap here because labour is not that cheap, but its getting cheaper as our standard of living drops. Soon we will be able to make it cheaper than they can as we pass each other on the stairs.

Large retailers are creeping the prices up of cheaply made foreign toasters so that you can now chose to pay £5 or £25, whichever you prefer, for such a toaster. Sainsbury's for example, with their different "ranges", like to cater for all pockets. This means of course that the retailer is taking up all the slack in the price, as profit. A toaster made using labour that costs 5% of British labour costs, sold at the same as a British made toaster, provides a very nice profit indeed. And when domestic production is floored after decades of this, there is no *immediate* chance of recovery.

The foreign manufacturer, not being stupid, and noticing that his wholesale customers are pushing up their prices, will push his up too. And he can afford to because there is no domestic manufacturer to produce an alternative. The destruction of British manufacture leaves the way open for foreign manufacturers to eventually push their prices up and not fear competition. The British consumer eventually won't even have cheap goods as a compensation for unemployment and national decline. When that time comes we will look up and realise that we have been pushed into poor nation status, unable to afford the no longer "cheap" goods we sold our domestic industry for. What will we do then?

Exploitation and the environmental aspects of goods produced by cheap foreign labour.

It is surprising how little people seem to be bothered by the knowledge that their clothes and other goods are often produced using exploited labour, including child labour. There has been no shortage of information over the past 3 decades about the conditions of low paid workers in foreign countries, but it has not stopped producers who use such labour leading the field in fashion clothing, often based on a young enlightened image which they sell to consumers. Asian men die of lung disease from sandblasting clothes so that westerners can walk around in jeans with that "worn out look". The same half-educated middle class left-wingers are capable of talking about Victorian exploitation, standing clothed in garments made by sweated child labour - abroad. Modern Britain hasn't abolished child labour, that was done slowly by Victorians and then Edwardians. Modern Britons have re-introduced it - abroad. Apparently foreign children don't count.

The same goes for pollution. By letting our goods be manufactured abroad we have merely exported our pollution to places where it isn't as regulated.

If anyone reading this book thinks that a return to manufacturing would mean more pollution, they should think how much pollution is created manufacturing their goods in China. Anything produced here would be subject to British standards of emissions control. The more we produce here the less global pollution there would be.

Higher wages keep money in the country.

People mistakenly think that the link between exports and wages is the important one, thinking that we mustn't pay ourselves high wages because we can't "afford it". But people often don't have the same anxiety about the profits of huge corporations actually leaving the country. Money paid to workers in the form of wages *stays in the economy*. Money creamed off in profits, if it is then invested abroad, is actually leaving the economy, and only part of it returns, later if ever, in the form of interest on the loans. But if those corporations making the profits are foreign-owned, then the money is gone forever. And the less we manufacture ourselves, the more likely those corporations are to be foreign owned, and it is a situation that grows worse unless reversed, as the flood of outward investment inevitably grows as British companies fade away. This flood of outward investment has continued since 1983 so that investment abroad has replaced domestic manufacture as a source of income.

The collapse of domestic manufacture has made even periods of prosperity a cause of further collapse.

British manufacture has so far collapsed across the whole range of products that the weakness of domestic production functions like a built in economic failure mechanism, as any increase in wages and spending spells a more than temporary worsening trade deficit. This is because even in normal circumstances, a spending boom (such as would follow substantial wage rises for the low paid) would result in a surge of imports as domestic production struggles to meet the increase in demand. This would lead to an even greater balance of payments deficit. When domestic production is completely lacking in large sectors, then the effect is total and permanent, as there is simply no domestic production there to recover. For this reason the ideal public response to higher wages would be: paying off personal debt, then saving, then spending in that order.

Unemployment and the Trade Deficit

Look at the plight of the lowest, worst off of the working classes, and there you will see the eventual plight of the nation as a whole. Their unemployment is Britain's future downfall.

The vital link is between what you use and what you import. We are importing most of what we use (We have a £8bn monthly deficit in manufactured goods, made up for by our money exports and "financial services" so that the net deficit is £4bn per month). And that can have only one long term result - poverty, for the whole nation. That really is living beyond our means (as we have to borrow money, or sell assets, to buy what we use), while investing in foreign firms to finance them to *make* what we use, to make what we have to buy from them. It doesn't take much to realise that it makes much better economic sense to lend money to British firms so that we can ourselves make what we use (and get a return on *that* investment). No matter how much we starve ourselves of wages from *the money we earn for our employers*, just so that they can invest it abroad, we still won't ever solve the failure of our economy until we get to work making what we use. It is the the unemployed who are the potential for our salvation, if they can be put to work manufacturing - for domestic use, to replace imports, *or* for export to earn money for imports. ***It is those 3 million pairs of hands that can dig us out of debt.***

For that to happen we have to invest in British industry. That means that the money that has accrued in the banks from our savings, or from the profits which are the fruits of our labours, has to be invested in new and existing British firms, to expand our manufacturing base.

How can we get the 500,000 to 700,000 unemployed 18-24 year olds to work?

We can tell them to get on their bikes and look for the jobs that don't exist, as Thatcher's Tories did.

Or we can try to subsidise youth employment schemes, to get them to work, no matter in what job, no matter how unskilled or low paid or otherwise useless to the national economy, as long as it's a job, as successive governments have done.

Or we can take other measures to harness these idle hands to Britain's recovery. To do so we have to acknowledge a few unpleasant facts:

1.There is an unwillingness of the banks to invest in new British companies. 2.Many young people leave school so badly educated that they are more or less unemployable. The education system, even at so called university level, and even in engineering courses, is failing to produce people who can provide an intelligent and able workforce to enable a British recovery to take place, especially in engineering.

So, we have to ensure that there is sufficient investment in new and existing industries to expand Britain's manufacturing. This means significant changes in the banking system. The deposits of small investors and account holders, should be used to fund loans to local businesses. This would mean their funds would no longer go to investment banking which has not served the needs of small to medium British companies.

Looking to large foreign companies to build assembly plants for cheap labour, as governments have been satisfied to do in the past, is not the way forwards for British industry or British workers, unless we want to stay poor and get poorer.

We also have to discard the recondite educational theories of the middle class left, which have gone so far in destroying the chance of working class pupils to achieve even a decent basic level of education. We should involve industry, big and small, and practising teachers, in forming education policy. It has to be said that the middle class Labour Party and their education advisors of the last decades are chiefly responsible for the destruction of education for the working classes. It is a destruction that plays a significant part in the decline of British industry.

A Board of Industrial Co-operation.

British industry has suffered from bad management, poor investment, bad education, poor pay and industrial unrest, and an overall lack of common purpose; we need to co-ordinate and co-operate in four sectors:
1. Owners and management.
2. Workers and unions.
3. Banks.
4. The education establishment (schools, universities and colleges).

One way to achieve this would be to create a "Board of Industrial Cooperation" which would meet to co-ordinate the needs of the sectors; this board would only have a consultative role but it provide continuity and could serve to focus public scrutiny on governments' attention to planning.

A similar body, (but with just trade unions and managers) has been in operation with great success in Austria since the 1970s. Essentially, the idea is that representatives from the different sectors meet to discuss their likely needs for the coming years, and co-ordinate how these needs can be fullfilled. A chief feature is that their findings have to be unanimous, which means of course that there is compromise. The strength of findings that are the result of compromise is that all the involved parties are content with them and more likely to deliver on the agreed aims. In Austria the role of this body is greatly expanded from its original conception, and plays a central role in policy making. In Britain we wouldn't want to go as far as they have in Austria because of the way it encroaches on Parliamentary Sovereignty(although we haven't minded giving that away to the EU) but a body of this kind, tailored to British expectations, could introduce a much needed consensus into policy making where we tend to suffer from short-termism, and a lack of planning and co-ordination. This lack of co-ordination has blighted the possibility of British industrial success and recovery since the end of the Second World War. Consensus and planning could revolutionise the British economy more than the notion of a board of industrial co-operation may suggest at first sight. This suggestion, including as it does more sectors than the Austrian model, has in some ways even greater potential.

In Sweden, for example, vocational courses are created in direct response to shortages in the workforce reported by industry. These courses in their turn are linked directly to jobs. This is a more direct approach to the labour market and education than just allowing the market forces to belatedly reveal to the hoards of media studies graduates that the few real job vacancies are filled and that they would have been better off doing another course.

Reliable and cheap finance for small and medium companies.

Mass production industries rely on the network of smaller engineering firms to support them and a properly educated workforce to operate them. Without these the profitable aspects of production are done abroad. That's what happened to the British car industry, which finally collapsed. To enable small British businesses to start up again and to expand we need to get money out of the banks and into society. Since the large banks no longer do much of what is called "traditional banking", lending depositors' savings to local businesses, this may involve breaking up the larger banks or introducing small local savings banks to finance local firms. A similar system funded post-war German growth, and ensured a continued prosperity after the initial recovery with Marshall Aid, and made Germany the leading economy in Europe, and the most successful exporter in the world (the country with the largest net exports *Source: WTO*). Publicly owned banks ought to be already doing it.

The negative role of the banks.

Our future prosperity depends on that investment, and so does the prosperity of the banks - unless they see it depending on their investments in foreign firms, investments basically in Britain's decline. The logic of that position is that finally there will only be one sort of British company left, British overseas investment banks - we the population would be their unemployed clients, paying each other pittances for services. Eventually we would be unable to afford to buy our televisions.

Such an unproductive and negative role of banking is not sustainable. The reputation of the banks has declined to its disastrous position as a result of this role. We have all seen that as well as being harmful to the long term prospects of our economy, it is not even profitable to the banks themselves. The tax payer has had to bail them out, at huge wasteful cost. It was only a lack of vision of any alternative that prevented us from letting them go to the wall. The new plans to encourage lending by guarantees from government who effectively buy up the loans the banks give is simply another form of government subsidy to the banks - another ill-judged, but this time covert, gift from the tax-payer to the super rich.

Banks that are part of the plan for our future prosperity. Small High Street Savings Banks

Industry then, especially small to medium sized industry, needs a new type of bank. Banks that are part of the community, part of the nation, and part of the plan for our future prosperity. Those that cannot participate in that should be let to fall by the wayside, we cannot afford them, they are a drain on the economy. Banks transcend national borders in their self interest. They have grown, too big to fail in the opinion of some, but also too big to be of any value within society. Many of the public thought that the failed banks should have been allowed to collapse.

The disaster that befell banking as a consequence of departing from traditional banking and seeking high risk profits elsewhere, for example in derivatives, was predicted by, for example, Franklin D Edwards, of Columbia University, NY, as early as 1993. In an article, *The Decline of Traditional Banking: Implications for Financial Stability and Regulatory Policy (Franklin R. Edwards and Frederic S. Mishkin)*.

He wrote;

"The traditional banking business has been to make long-term loans and fund them by issuing short-dated deposits, a process that is commonly described as "borrowing short and lending long." In recent years, fundamental economic forces have undercut the traditional role of banks in financial intermediation. As a source of funds for financial intermediaries, deposits have steadily diminished in importance. In addition, the profitability of traditional banking activities such as business lending has diminished in recent years. As a result, banks have increasingly turned to new non-traditional financial activities as a way of maintaining their position as financial intermediaries.

A key policy issue is whether the decline of banking threatens to make the financial system more fragile. If nothing else, the prospect of a mass exodus from the banking industry (possibly via increased failures) could cause instability in the financial system. Of greater concern is that declining profitability could tip the incentives of bank managers toward assuming greater risk in an effort to maintain former profit levels. For example, banks might make loans to less creditworthy borrowers or engage in non-traditional financial activities that promise higher returns but carry greater risk. A new activity that has generated particular concern recently is the expanding role of banks as dealers in derivatives products. There is a fear that in seeking new sources of revenue in derivatives, banks may be taking risks that could ultimately undermine their solvency and possibly the stability of the banking system."

The scale of trading in derivatives is hard to comprehend. Derivatives, by the way, are entities such as futures that are not connected to commodities with actual values. In other words, "they do not have any intrinsic value in themselves" *(Source: Christopher Esposito, The Dangers of Financial Derivatives).*

The world trade in derivatives is estimated to be in the region of $600 trillion. To put that figure into perspective, think that the World GDP (the Gross Domestic Product of all the countries added together) for a year is only $68 trillion. No wonder banks can't be bothered to invest in small local businesses.

Some of their bubbles have burst but there are a lot more, and bigger, bubbles to follow.

In the meantime, away from the world of the super rich, where the rest of us live, the real world of jobs and work and man hours producing what we need and what we use depends still on investment in businesses, on a small scale. A different future for banking then would lie in investment in domestic industry. The new higher wage economy would produce a store of savings, ready to be invested through small high street banks. One way of creating these is for government to force the break up of different banking functions to create new small local banks. This change can grow out of a new public awareness of the vital need for investment, of the crisis facing us. The old banks have proved that we need new banks.

Pensions

The enormous cost of pensions and of health care for an ageing population is a worry for the future. It is another reason to ask if we can *afford* to keep the bottom 8 million of the population in poverty, on low wages or in unemployment, for their working lives before they are old and need expensive hip replacements and heart operations, when they could be contributing to the coffers to pay for what is going to be necessary. Can we *afford* to keep 8 million so poor that they are not paying much tax and are perhaps even a net drain on the Treasury because they are claiming in-work benefits to get by? Can we *afford* to allow employers to pay so little that the wages they pay are subsidised by the Treasury? If we are worried about the pensions and health care of the future, hadn't we better invest in British industry and training to make sure that the bottom 8 million are earning the money to pay for it all? And hadn't we better make sure that their wages are high enough to enable them to both live and pay tax? Alternatively we can let the big corporations keep the money. But who is going to pay for the hip replacements? Tesco? Or the Chinese and German companies who receive the profits in the form of investments?

Many of those living in poverty in Britain today are pensioners. The problem facing any government is: how can the country afford to pay our pensioners what we would like to? We cannot eradicate poverty unless we make sure that pensioners without company pensions get more than they are getting, so that they can afford enough food and heating, and have something left over for leisure, and to live reasonably comfortably. While raising the revenue (£74bn *Source: Dept. of Works and Pensions*) to pay 7 million pensioners their £144 per week may be a headache to any government, it is not really a national economic problem, except that the elderly are unable to make much of a contribution any more to the nation's wealth (they have already done so of course). It isn't all that much of a problem since, being poor many of them, they spend the money they get almost immediately on food, and heating. So the money goes straight back into the economy (i.e. not to imports). This only becomes a problem if the huge corporations who own all the retail food outlets then take the money and invest it abroad, thereby sending all that money out of the country; out of the country to fund foreign industries to make the grandchildren of the pensioners unemployed so that they can't earn the money to pay for their own pensions and those of their parents and grandparents. It also matters if British energy companies can't offer the best deals to pensioners so that foreign companies get their accounts and the money leaves the country that way. It becomes easier to raise pensions when the haemorrhage of money from the country is stopped. A working class government would have to have a commitment to increasing pensions enough to eradicate poverty in that age group. Saving on the £60bn in-work benefits, putting 8 million further above the tax threshold who are currently on low pay, and investing in British manufacture so that we are making what we need and not absorbing unemployment benefit, are ways to raise money for better pensions without increased taxation rates.

Wouldn't a high minimum wage put a strain on public services, notably the NHS?

It would increase the wages bill, because the hospital porters and cleaners for example are currently paid less than the minimum wage proposed here. It would cost roughly another £3 billion per year (the NHS budget is currently £97bn). It would be more than paid for by the increased tax receipts from the 8 million currently low paid workers in the private sector. Remember too that, because government is usually paying out that £60bn housing benefit and other benefits to low paid workers, the net cost of higher wages in the public sector such as the NHS would be offset partly by that substantial saving. In other words if a hospital porter is earning £16,000 pa and getting maybe £200 per month in housing benefit, then his increased salary of £19,400, a rise of £3,400 can be partly offset by the £2,400pa government would save on his housing benefit, as well as savings on housing benefits to private sector workers.

An impoverished population is a heavy burden on the National Health Service. For all parties, the NHS is a bottomless pit in terms of funding, there is no limit really to how much money the nation could spend on it. Any money spent on it would make life better for each one of us at some time in our lives. It is one of the chief elements of the welfare state that has improved the quality of life for the poor.

Unemployment benefit, housing benefit, the prison service, the police, and the NHS, are effectively subsidising the low paying corporations. Employers need a more or less healthy workforce to create their profits for them, but they do not pay enough for many of their workers to live healthily. And the cost of repairing their ill health is borne by the NHS. Poverty brings health problems. If people were better paid and better able to look after themselves they wouldn't need so much attention from the NHS. Good food, better housing and a better way of life prolongs health. The middle classes live longer than the working classes. If there were a high minimum wage, the result would be a lighter burden on the NHS, so the money we already spend on it would go further. The effect would be equivalent to an increase in funding.

A nation that doesn't pay its own way cannot in the long run give itself a high standard of health care.

If we *don't* take these measures, if we don't get rid of the low wage economy, the future for the NHS, as well as for the nation as a whole, looks bleak in the long term. As we get poorer and become the low wage packers and assemblers of foreign goods, as we slowly become in effect similar to a third world country, we will naturally be less able to afford the level of health care we have come to expect. Because of the huge budget deficit, £120bn, coupled with a £1200bn debt, this could be just around the corner; there will simply not be the money to pay for the NHS as is it today, and as the population gets poorer and less healthy, the burden upon a less well funded health service will eventually be overwhelming. We ought to be worried about the future of the health service. The danger does not come from politicians, but from our own refusal to face the hard facts about paying our own way. No-one is going to pay for our health service for us - we as a country have to earn the money to pay for it.

*

Removal from the European Union.

The EU is the largest unelected regime in the world outside China.

"2010 was the last time you will elect a government. From now on, the government will be civil servants and ex-politicians, from this country and abroad, whom I, and the Prime Ministers of other European countries, will appoint. Their experience in government makes them suitable for the job and there is no need to submit their ideas to the electorate. There is no longer any need to elect the

*government. There will still be elections for MPs, but that
won't effect who the government is. Any objections? And by
the way the Queen is willing to sign her approval to this"*

Imagine if the present Prime Minister said the above; You'd
think that you were having a nightmare. Or you'd think
treason was afoot, and that the Prime Minister and Her
Majesty had gone mad, and were trying to wipe away the
democracy that had been achieved over the slow march of 750
years or so. (Don't worry, as you read on, I won't make up a
quote again, the rest are real, unfortunately).

But that is what is being proposed. Not just proposed, that
is what is being done, it is being made into a fact, while
Britain sleeps and while our own politicians lie to us and
cheat us about it. They will do what they can to stop a
referendum on whether Britain not only loses its self
government, but decides to put itself under what is an
unelected regime, the Government of the EU, **the
Commission**. The same fate is befalling the other 400
million people of Europe, as we all become subject to the vast
unelected administrative dictatorship that the people of
Europe do not want. Don't let the benign pale blue face of the
EU fool you. The EU is the darkest cloud to cover Europe
since the spread of Nazism and the Communist Bloc that
followed in its wake.

The EU is *not* the people or countries of Europe, it is not a
country, it is an organisation, it is a group of the elite
international governing class of administrators who seek, in
the most spectacular coup d'état, to replace the democracies

85

of the various peoples of Europe with with the rule of their own administrative elite class, to replace it with their own organisation, and call it a state. You can get rid of a government, but an administration is permanent.

They have managed to supersede many of the laws of the European countries with the rules and aims of their organisation. They have repeatedly, insofar as they have been able, refused to allow the people of Europe to vote on whether they accept this scheme, because when they are allowed to vote in referendums on it, they vote against it. This group of the administrative elite, are quite unrelated to, because not actually elected by, the peoples of Europe. (In case you didn't know, the government of the EU is not taken from the elected MEPs, see below).

Jose Barosso, the current President of the EU Commission

A former Maoist, he says that **"The EU is an antidote to democratic governments"**. In his view government is best left to the experts; democracy, the people, cannot be trusted. As he points out;**"Decisions taken by the most democratic institutions in the world are very often wrong"**. No doubt. How fortunate then that the EU is not a democracy.

Fortunate too then, that in Barosso's words **"a federal Europe will be a reality in a few years"** (largely because they won't let the people of Europe vote on it).

In other words, we in Britain, for example, will no longer be in a democracy but part of a state *without an elected government,* called the European Union - an *unelected* government, but with all the power of an elected government.

One reason why people don't react to this, is that the large influential group of the middle class left think of the EU as a benign, well-intentioned organisation, likely to introduce the kind of measures a social democrat government might. This influential class of people, who control large parts of the media, especially television, don't mind if there is a "democratic deficit" (which is how the EU itself refers to the fact that its government is unelected). The EU might be a non-elected government but it seems to be vaguely left wing, so the left don't mind it. These are people who think that getting what they think is their own way at the ballot box is more important than democracy itself. If they can bypass democracy and get the kind of middle of the road social measures they favour then all well and good. There are many left wing Europeans, who are sceptical about democracy, who have nothing at all against by-passing it, or getting rid of it. There are many left wing people in Britain too who have the same attitude. Sometimes if you protest about the EU being non-democratic, people say "but what good is democracy anyway, it gave us... this horrible government I don't like" (whatever that government might be). Or they point to the flaws and failings, they say "look at the MPs' expenses scandal" and think that is a reason to abandon democracy, not realising how much worse it would be *without* democracy. (No need to even bother talking about the EU gravy-train here).

At some point we have to decide if we really do want to accept a "benign" dictatorship, to have our decisions made for us by experts. If we do want that then it is a very serious step to take, with very serious potential consequences. And if not, if we decide we *don't* want to accept that democracy is abolished or seriously weakened in Europe, then we have to leave the EU.

A few Q&As about the EU and democracy:

Q *What is meant by "unelected" and "not democratic" ? Is this an exaggeration?*

A. The EU is not a democracy, the government of the EU is not democratically elected.

Q *What is the Government of the EU*

A The Government (the executive) of the EU is called the Commission.

Q *Isn't that elected?*

A No it is appointed.

Q *Who appoints it?*

A The Prime Ministers of the member states.

Q *So what are the EU elections about then?*

A They elect the MEPs.

Q *And what do they do?*

A The MEPs sit in the European Parliament

Q *Doesn't that mean it's a democracy then?*

A No, because the European Parliament doesn't form the government of the EU, and no MEPs are in the government. There has so far been no connection whatsoever between the European Parliament and the EU government.

Q So when we have an election for the MEPs, that doesn't change the government?

A No

Q How come?

A It was never intended to. The MEPs, the parliament, are just a consultative body. Also they give an impression of democracy. After all, people expect there to be a parliament of come kind. People just presume it has something to do with the government. This one doesn't. It's what you could call a rubber stamp.

Q So what's all that about the European parliament making so and so many 100 laws per week.

A It's not true. They don't make any. They *approve* them.

Q So who makes them then?

A The Commission, the Commission is the government.

Q And the Commission is just appointed?

A That's right.

Q How long has this been going on?

A Twenty years.

The good news is that after the 2014 elections next year, the EU is going to make a gesture towards rectifying what they euphemistically call the "democratic deficit". For they are well aware of the dangers of the 450 million people they govern finding out finally despite years of lying and deceiving, that the EU is not a democracy. After the elections in May 2014 the European parliament is going to be allowed to put forwards their own suggestion for the leader of the Commission, called the President of the Commission. This is a very exciting moment for the EU as it is the first time since its beginning, that there has been any sort of democratic link between the parliament and the government; a really interesting experiment for them, bringing them out of the middle ages right into the early 18th century. Who knows, maybe by the time our children's children are voting the EU might go the whole way. They may for example introduce the idea of a prospective government having to put their proposals before the 450 million people who form the European Union electorate, to try to get their votes, like in a real election. However, there is a strong opposition to that idea. Many of the highest Eurocrats believe that involving the electorate in determining policy (what we would normally call *democracy*) would undermine the workings of the EU. They believe that party politics would be a bad thing for the EU, as it would mean that instead of getting the best policies for Europe, decided by those who know best, there would be the intrusion of the electorate's opinion.

There is another somewhat important question on which they feel it is dangerous to ask the electorate's opinion; and that is the question of whether they want to be in the EU at all. Whenever they have been asked in any of the member states they keep saying no. The EU therefore does what it can to avoid the national governments holding referendums.

You would think that the United Nations might have something to say about whether 450 million people should be allowed a plebiscite to decide what nation they want to be part of?

Why Don't Eurocrats like Democracy?

It is no mere accident that the EU isn't democratic and that the EU government doesn't have to present its programme before the people of Europe in an election. The architects of the EU are not democrats, (and it has nothing to do with the fact that some of the best of of them have been rejected at the ballot box in their own countries). They believe that government is best left to the experts, to administrators. They think that policy is too important to be left to the people to decide. The distance between the Commissioners and public opinion is by design. The intention is that the Commissioners can make the best decisions unhampered by what the ignorant public may think. To these administrators, democracy is akin to demagoguery. This is a view the merits of which we ought to consider; after all, what does the public know of economics or the EU, social policy, or the law? Or democracy? Relying on expert administrators is naturally the path advocated by....the expert administrators who are the Eurocrats. It is perfectly rational therefore to keep democracy at a distance from the government of Europe. The architects of Europe perhaps mistrust the people of Europe on account of the widespread popularity of various forms of fascism in Europe in the 1930s, in Germany, Austria, Hungary, Finland, France, Italy, Spain, Greece, Romania, Lithuania. It is a shame the same history doesn't teach them to mistrust the *abolition* of democracy, a rather well known feature of fascism.

This is what Tony Benn describes;

"When I was president of the EEC council of energy ministers for 6 months in 1977, I used to sit and look at my colleagues around the table...I was the only minister there who had not lived under fascism or Nazism or been occupied by the Germans. For them the EEC represents an incredible liberation from a memory of oppression and war, while for us it was a derogation of our historic democratic right to select and remove our governments"*(Parliament, People and Power 1982)*.

The historical popularity of fascism in Europe is another reason to urge British caution when getting entangled with large anti-democratic European movements such as the EU.

All hopes of political change within our country, all political aspirations of any kind, from any party, will be made impossible when the unelected EU government gradually and finally takes over from our democratically elected parliament. If we value our freedom, if we have any desire for change within our country, we must oppose the EU.

If we do not leave the EU we are consigning ourselves to decades during which generations will grow up with lower expectations of what democracy should be. Pretty soon there will be a generation who can't remember democracy - then it will be lost.

If this programme of greater pay equality seems difficult to achieve, for example, imagine how difficult it will be when there is no functioning democracy, when there is only an unreachable class of administrators designing the rules of capitalism by which their 450 vassals must live. And one of their primary purposes is to make cheap labour easy to move across borders to make it available to capitalists.

The EU, labour and immigration

When the working classes complain that immigrants from Europe come to Britain and take their jobs, the middle classes sneer at them (call them racists too), and say "but British workers won't even do those jobs", and what they mean is, "they won't even do those jobs *for the money we want to pay them*, so we'll get someone who will".

The EU is built upon 4 pillars. They are presented as something to do with liberty but it is in fact the freedom of movement of the essentials of capitalism; the Free Movement of Goods, Free Movement of Capital, Free Movement of Services, Free Movement of People. EU law allows for the free movement of workers between countries, and makes restrictions illegal (except those allowed by EU law). The EU law is explicit; workers have the right to reside and be employed and unemployed in any member state of their choice under the same conditions as those enjoyed by citizens of that country (except where EU law allows for them to be paid less, see below). Free movement of labour across a territory with such differences in standards of pay creates perfect conditions of employment for employers, and they have availed themselves of this and other EU legislation to get the most out of their workers for the minimum possible. The EU is an employers' charter.

To start with, a company can bring their own workers with them, and the EU can be used as extra legal muscle against union action, as British oil workers found out in 2009 at the Lindsay oil refinery. British workers who hadn't even been allowed to apply for the jobs there, were branded racists and xenophobes for.....wanting jobs (Denis MacShane, *The Guardian* 2nd Feb 2009, Mary Riddel, *The Daily Telegraph* 4th Feb 2009. For a different view see Labour MP John Cruddas also in *The Guardian* 31st Jan 2009). The workers were protesting that jobs in Britain were given to workers from abroad (these weren't immigrants, but workers brought by the company). The British Prime Minister himself was forced to backtrack after piping up vainly for "British jobs" finding that he had fallen foul of EU law, having forgotten that the EU was designed specifically to allow employers to employ workers *from* wherever they want, *wherever* they want.

Recently the EU allowed a restriction on the immigration of Romanian workers, which has now expired. The restriction was allowed (not only in "xenophobic" Britain, as middle class commentators loved to call it, but also in "xenophobic" Spain, France, Austria, Belgium, the Netherlands, and Germany. Obviously the sudden influx of some of the EU's poorest workers would have given the game away. Now however, that influx can be expected, and we are used to the idea. We ought to be in no doubt that in the long run, significant movements of peoples are expected. Nor should we doubt what the purpose of it is. As the Telegraph put it; "the native population (of Lincolnshire) had no inclination to harvest cabbages" (at the rates paid to the migrant workers) "who worked for £25 per day...and paid £80 per week rent to live 20 people in a room... We should be grateful to them for our prosperity" (for the prosperity of the gang masters and Tesco higher up the food chain). Low Pay Britain is a proud asset for the Europhile middle classes.

In Sweden, where the trade unions have ensured high wages for the working classes, which is the reason why there is no poverty in Sweden of the kind we have to endure here, the EU courts were used to sweep aside collective bargaining. In the case of Laval Un Partneri v Svenska Byggnadsarbetar förbundet (The Swedish Building Workers Union), a Romanian company was able to make imported workers work for less than Swedish workers, despite the efforts of the Swedish Union; a strike was ruled illegal and the union fined. There was a similar judgement in Luxembourg, and another in Finland.

The EU Posted Workers Directive has meant that workers can be moved into a country by a company which only has to pay the wages they might have received *in their country of origin*. The only stipulation is that it meets minimum wage laws of the new country. In other words, the working classes can only defend the *minimum* wage against the EU, no other wages. This Directive is aimed against trade unions. If we cannot leave the EU, then this is another reason why we had better make sure that we have a high National Minimum Wage. If we have a low one, that is the one immigration will be used to push us down to. Logically it can mean that they can flood the labour market with low paid European workers until we are *all* on £6 per hour. (It is even harder for newly arrived immigrants to survive on £6 per hour than it is with British workers with family networks and a certain degree of support and familiarity with their surroundings. Imagine living in an alien environment on so little, and getting established. How do you find the deposit for a rental, for example? But if they are used to worse, they accept it).

And that is the whole thinking behind the EU; it is a capitalist organisation to ensure a plentiful supply of cheap labour where and when it is needed in order to drive down the wages of the working classes. The working classes of course include each successive wave of immigrants who, once they have become acclimatised and eventually settled in Britain, if they can manage that, also want to be paid a decent wage, and not have their wages driven down by a new wave of immigrants. It is at that point that they lose the sympathy of the left wing middle classes.

The future for the working classes of Europe is to be herded around and used as migratory labour, in barges and camps, as they were at the Lindsay oil refinery, and as they are all across Norfolk for example in gangers' sheds and barracks, used as cheap labour in one country then another, always to drive each other's wages down. The middle class left have been wrong-footed by their own obsession with racism (with which they obediently brand any working class opposition to classical capitalism) and cannot find a way to give voice to the working class anxiety over this growing menace to pay and conditions across the whole of Europe. The "xenophobia" chant is an equivalent to the divide and rule technique of the past. The working class movements of Europe need to unite to defeat it. The EU is a menace facing the low paid and better paid workers alike, across Europe.

When a Labour Prime Minister called a life long Labour supporter a "bigot" for asking about action on immigration from Europe, he demonstrated how far the Labour Party had drifted away from representing the interests of the working classes, and towards the middle class view of politics. But the EU is not only a capitalist organisation with a policy on labour that is designed to push working class wages down, it is also one that represents a coup d'etat against democracy, and establishes an unelected dictatorship by the administrative classes.

No referendum?

Our two main parties between them have contrived to arrange it so that each one promises a referendum *if* they are re-elected after a long term of government. If, as always happens, they are turned out, then there will be no referendum, and the next government then issues another promise further up the line until they are voted out, and so on. It is remarkable how stupid the present government think people are, when they posture as offering a referendum when in fact they are refusing one. They are insisting on 4 more years of EU progress, to see how near a *fait accompli* it can get. In the end there will be no more opportunity to choose.

The project outlined on this book is a political movement to change the functioning of capitalism in Britain - one of the most important steps is to preserve our democracy, our right to decide over our own lives.

.

The EU, how it works.

If people knew the facts about the European Union they would be worried about it. If it were suggested outright as a proposal it would be rejected, even violently opposed.

As it is, it is a sneaking change whose aims its proponents refuse to declare openly. It is a monumental political change which substantially reduces our democracy. But because it is done bit by bit, and because they have repeatedly denied intentions which they then later carry out, opposition never forms against it as it otherwise would.

Most people don't know how the European Union is structured. There follows below a very brief outline. Read this, or in any other way you can (by visiting the European Union's own web site for example) try to find out how the European Union works, as it can and does make laws which *you have to obey.*

THERE ARE THREE MAIN PARTS of the European Union. The parliament is only one third of the structure. There are two other bodies more powerful than the parliament.

1 The **EUROPEAN COUNCIL** (or sometimes called the Council of Ministers). These are the Prime Ministers of the member states. This is where the main general policy decisions are made {There are other smaller summits, of say, the Environment Ministers of each of the member states, or the Foreign Ministers and so on, and these are called the Environment Council, Foreign Council etc. But when it is the Prime Ministers this is called the EUROPEAN COUNCIL}.

This Council of Prime Ministers is the main decision making body. They make all the decisions about the direction the European Union will take. These are the areas these councils cover;

General Affairs
Foreign Affairs
Economic and Financial Affairs (ECOFIN)
Justice and Home Affairs (JHA)
Employment, Social Policy, Health and Consumer Affairs
Competitiveness
Transport, Telecommunications and Energy
Agriculture and Fisheries
Environment
Education, Youth and Culture

How they actually vote is that each country carries a certain number of votes according to its population. Except in the areas of tax, immigration, asylum, security and foreign policy, where voting has to be unanimous, a majority of 255 out of 345 carries the vote, as long as it "represents" 62% of the population of the European Union (none of whom have been consulted on the policies implemented, or had them presented to them in an election campaign).

Each minister in these councils is taken as having the full authority of his country, that is, of his government and his parliament (even though he doesn't), and therefore his people (even though he doesn't). His signature on an act is binding and becomes law, which must be obeyed in all countries in the European Union.

2 THE EUROPEAN COMMISSION

The Commission is the executive, the government of the EU. This is the body which actually drafts the *laws* to govern all the European Union territories in the policy areas listed above.

{To Compare; In Britain, and in most other parliamentary democracies, it is Parliament which makes these laws, and Parliament is dominated by the party which has won the most seats in a general election. In the EU the Commission is akin to both our parliament and our executive (government), see below}.

But the Commission is <u>not elected.</u>

This COMMISSION is a body of 27 people, one from each member state, who are however *appointed* by the Council of Ministers, and stay in office for 5 years. This appointment has been made for 20 years without even the slightest hint of democracy interfering in it. After 2014, the MEPs will have a chance to select their own candidates for the post of *President* of the Commission (see **Post 2014**, below)

At present Britain's appointee is Baroness Ashton. Previous Commissioners from Britain have included Neil Kinnock, John Patten, Leon Brittan and Peter Mandelson. None of these were ever accepted by the electorate as Prime Ministers, and yet they quietly wielded one 27th part of dictatorial power in Europe, with no need to ever refer to the electorate or to public opinion in any way.

The Commissioners are expected to be independent of their countries and to instead uphold the interests of the European Union as a whole, rather than the interests of their own countries.

These 27 appointed people, *not the parliament* are the only body with the power to draft proposals for laws, which they then present to the Council and then to the European Parliament (see below) for approval. They are responsible for drafting the budget and for implementing the European Union's laws and programmes, and spending its funds.

3 The **EUROPEAN PARLIAMENT**

This is where the Euro MPs sit (MEPs) and they are elected in the Euro elections once every 5 years.

The European Union elections are not related in any way to the government of the EU. This is not where the government of the EU sits, and the government of the EU has never come from the European Parliament.

There are 735 seats, each country having seats in proportion to its population.

The parliament's role is largely consultative. Unlike our parliament, *it does NOT at present control or determine in any way, the executive.* It has to be consulted and has the choice to give assent to a proposed law, or to reject it. In some cases only it has the right to ask for amendments. More recently a system called Co-decision is being used for most EU legislation, to give parliament more power, *supposedly but not* equal to the Council.

Most importantly, the European Parliament *is not sovereign* (as Westminster is).

4. Along with these bodies is the **EUROPEAN COURT OF JUSTICE**, which is responsible for enforcing the laws made by the European Union. Any country found to be breaking one of these laws can be heavily fined and this way the laws are imposed.

Criticisms;

In the interests of free trade, within Europe, we are being asked to accept dramatic reductions in our democratic rights. Customarily capitalism is associated with democracy and freedom - Since when has it been necessary to give away democracy just to be able to trade?

Remember, the whole purpose of the European Union is supposed to be economic. Never has it been proposed to the people as a political proposal, uniting Britain with European Countries in a federation (a state such as the United States of America) or any other arrangement. Indeed any such idea has always been *strenuously denied* by the British politicians in favour of British membership. They will go on denying it...until it is a fact. In Europe however the federalist intention is no mere suspicion, it has always been the intention, and it remains the long term aim of European officials. It may take them some time more to achieve it, but it is not an intention that will go away. British opposition to it is regarded as a temporary hurdle which will eventually be overcome or simply got around. Concealing the federalist intention from the British people is routine for them. A kind of joke.

Why a treaty instead of a constitution?

There is no constitution of the EU, it is held together with treaties. This is for one good reason; a constitution needs referendums, treaties don't.

A treaty can be signed by Prime Ministers without reference to the people. But these aren't normal treaties, these are treaties that give away sovereignty, that change the constitutional realities of the countries concerned.

That is what happened when they were planning the Lisbon Treaty. Initially they had intended to have a constitution, until it was rejected by both the French and the Dutch people in referendums; they realised that for the British Prime Minister to sign a constitution he would have to give the British people a referendum too; So they scrapped that idea and replaced it with a treaty, which a British Prime Minister, and other Prime Ministers, could sign without an election or referendum; a deliberate trick to prevent the people of Europe from having a say over their destiny.

Valerie Giscard D' Estaing is an ex French President and chairman of the committee which drew up the constitution. He maybe has an instinct for imperial pan-Europeanism, being a descendant of Louis XV and Charlemagne. He was accused in France of accepting diamonds from Bokassa, the fleeing dictator of Central African Republic to whom D'Estaing had given military aid, who had looted his own treasury of millions. He confirmed that the Lisbon Treaty was "almost the same" as the previously proposed constitution which had been rejected in French and Dutch referendums.

"The Treaty of Lisbon is the same as the rejected constitution. Only the format has been changed to avoid referendums".

He himself acknowledged that **"public opinion will be led to adopt, without knowing it, the proposals which we dare not present to them directly"** and **"all the proposals will be in the new text but will be hidden and disguised in some way".**

He conceded that this **"would confirm to European citizens the notion that European construction is a procedure organised behind their backs by lawyers and diplomats."** (*Le Monde 15 June 2007.*)

What they did was to take the controversial aspects of the Constitution and spread it out in treaties to conceal it. This is deception on a staggering scale, a political coup d'etat against the democracies representing 450 million people. A coup carried out by the elite class of administrators and politicians who feel justified in their deception because they know best. Is this too bad to be true? Hard to believe? This is what Gisgard D'Estaing said himself;

"They have taken the original draft constitution, blown it apart into separate elements, and have then attached them, one by one, to existing treaties. The Treaty of Lisbon is thus a catalogue of amendments. It is unpenetrable for the public."

And where did he make this startling statement? Was it whispered on the back stairs of an EU building? Overheard by an undercover reporter? No, he wrote it in an article in the Independent newspaper, 30th October 2007. Read it online for yourself.

Of what significance is the "impenetrability" of the Treaty? This is what Jens Peter Bonde, the centre left Danish politician and MEP, author of over 60 books on the EU said about it;

"How can we be sure that none of them (the 27 Prime Ministers) had read what they signed? Very easily. The text is quite simply unreadable! In the French version there are 329 A4 pages of different and unconnected amendments to the 17 existing basic treaties. The amendments can only be read and understood if they are inserted at the appropriate places in the 2800 pages of relevant treaties. That is the only way in which to see what is amended and how. It is only after a comparison has been made that it is possible to understand the amendments and start to think about the consequences of implementing them. It does not take days but weeks to grasp the whole context, even for specialists"

Yes, the 27 Prime Ministers signed the Treaty of Lisbon without reading it.

<u>Guliano D'Amato</u>, He is Vice Chairman of the committee that framed the rejected EU constitution, and an ex-president of Italy, who served for one corruption-scandal ridden year. He served again during 2001 despite not being a member of parliament. After the term in office, dismissed by the electorate, he solemnly vowed to leave politics. He didn't however, and went on to a bright career in the EU, where electorates don't have to be faced. He said, at a meeting of the *Centre for European Reform* on 12 July 2007 that EU leaders **"decided that the document should be unreadable. . . In order to make our citizens happy, to produce a document that they will never understand!"** and **"The good thing about not calling it a Constitution is that no one can ask for a referendum on it."** - 21 February 2007.

Jean Claude Juncker Prime Minister of Luxembourg **"Britain is different. Of course there will be transfers of sovereignty. But would I be intelligent to draw the attention of public opinion to this fact?"** - (*Daily Telegraph 3 July 2007*).

Karel de Gucht, Belgian Foreign Minister **"The aim of the *Constitutional* treaty was to be more readable; the aim of *this* treaty is to be *un*readable...The Constitution aimed to be clear, whereas this treaty had to be unclear. It is a success."** - (*in Flandreinfo, 23 June 2007*).

As **Dr Garrat Fitzgerrald** explained in the Irish Times **They (the treaties) have simply been designed to enable certain heads of government to sell to their people the idea of ratification by parliamentary action rather than by referendum."** -(Irish Times, 30 June 2007.

Andrea Merkel, The German Chancellor makes her views very clear to the European Parliament;

"European integration has to be striven for and consolidated time and again."

The federalists who dominate in the EU do not care either that the populations of all the European countries which have enjoyed the courtesy of being asked in a referendum, have all shown their rejection of the idea. The federalists, if they feel the need to ask at all, will simply keep asking the same question until the answer is **yes.**

But their policy is to avoid referendums. And that is what the Lisbon Treaty was for.

But before we talk of paying the price.....

Is it any use in the first place?

The European Union's only justification for its existence is a practical one, to do with trade; And yet increasingly, and for the future, the European Union has no real useful purpose. Trade is now global. The multitude of rules and restrictions for which the European Union is notorious make competition with the eastern economies more difficult than it already is. The EU was set up to make trade *within Europe* easier, to lower trade barriers and to promote competition, and to provide cheap labour by removing immigration restrictions. In this aim it has been largely successful, at a cost to the working classes whose pay has been kept down. The EU has the opposite effect on competitiveness outside Europe.

The European Union is not democratic

The political cost we pay for lowering trade barriers inside Europe is a very high one. We have to accept an endless stream of new laws from a source completely outside of our democracy. We do not vote for the Commission of 27, it is appointed by the Prime Ministers. We only vote for the Parliament, which has only a very limited power, akin to the power our Parliament had... under the Tudors. *Unlike our own present day parliament, the government of the EU does not come from parliament.* **When we vote in the Euro elections for MEPs we are NOT voting for an EU government.** That is appointed. We are voting for the rubber stamp. Is it possible that the British people are willing to swap being governed by Parliament for being governed by appointees? Are the British people willing to go back hundreds of years in terms of their political rights?

Do the other European people even want it?

The European Union is not wanted by the other populations of Europe either. It is the project of the elite class of politicians and officials whose enthusiasm for it has driven right over the will of the peoples. Each time some aspect of their scheme, the Euro, or the new constitution, for example, is rejected by an electorate in a referendum, the plan is merely shelved until they will be asked again. Each nation will be asked again until they say "YES" to whatever they are asked to accept. Then, and only then, can you be assured they will be asked no more.

Twenty Seven Masters of Europe

The sheer amount of power given to the heads of state, in the European Council, (they appoint the 27 Commissioners who then frame the laws) is beyond the intention of the people electing them. In one room can be contained the 27 Prime Ministers, who can decide between them in principle the laws you and I, and 450 million other Europeans must obey and the direction the whole of Europe is to take. The EU is in effect the largest dictatorship in the world outside China. Such a process is like going back to absolute monarchy, with a rubber stamp parliament. Remember, in British politics, the Prime Minister is really merely the leader of the party with most votes in our parliament, until the next election. He is not intended to be the elected dictator to decide all our futures, along with a small group of other men in the same position in the other countries of Europe.

If a British minister, including a Prime Minister, wants to make a law he has to face parliament, but if he goes to Europe, he can push it through the Council of 27 likeminededs, never face parliament, and bingo! its a law.

European elections do not remove European legislators

The use of the words *European Parliament,* and *Elections*, give a wholly false impression, and invite a misleading association of ideas with a proper parliament. The European Parliament is not sovereign; it doesn't rule. We get rid of our national government if we want to, in an election. Euro-elections, on the other hand do NOT get rid of the government of Europe, because the government is not in the parliament. The EU government are the Commissioners appointed by the Council of Ministers; and the group of Prime Ministers themselves, in their role of controlling the European Union, govern without being accountable to a parliament.

You cannot change the direction of the European Union by voting

While after each European Election the MEPs (Members of European Parliament) change, the Commissioners, the actual legislators, are not changed. When they do change, the change *does not of course reflect the outcome of the election*, a new set of 27 appointees is put in their place, chosen in the same way, by the same Prime Ministers who chose the previous ones, and business proceeds as before. This happens 6 months after the election. They have merely coincided the new appointment with the time of elections to give the *impression* of democracy.

It is taken for granted that the Commissioners are "pro-European" in their opinions. That is what they are appointed for. No one is chosen to be a Commissioner if he is Euro-sceptic. Only one type of opinion is able to flourish and gain power in the European Union. We, the British electorate, cannot vote it away, just as it was put there with no reference to our opinions.

POST 2014

For the first time, after the 2014 elections, the MEPs will have the right to suggest candidates for the post of Commission President. But remember that the other 27 Commissioners will *still* be appointed and never have to face an electorate.

The question worrying the Eurocrats now is whether a partisan Commission President, one who has had to present his policies to parliament (but not to the people), can function in the same way as Commissioners have done before. Eurocrats tend to think that this tentative flirtation with democracy might spoil the free hand with which the EU Commission has been able to act until now. **"For the past 20 years, the heads of state and government have picked the Commission President from among their own group because they trust Prime Ministers who have experience in running large and complex administrations. The Commission's effectiveness depends critically on the President's ability to work with national leaders, and she (sic) would be taken more seriously by them if she is one of their peers"** *(Heather Grabbe, former senior advisor to the European Commissioner for Enlargement)* a precise and subtle description of a ruling class unused to interference from an electorate. The sad truth is that it will likely make little difference. The change is a belated move to try to correct the **democratic deficit** (the lack of democracy). It means that after 2014 the MEPs can have a say in the choice of dictator, the man who can rule Europe above the heads of the 450 million Europeans, the man who doesn't have to say one word to one single elector about his proposed policies. The abhorrence with which the Eurocrats regard the electorate makes it unlikely that the relationship between the Commissioner and the people will be any more direct than that.

And if you are still in any doubt about the degree of power the Commissioner has, then the new powers given to him ought to clear that up; **"Member-states have agreed that the Commission should monitor and enforce fiscal discipline across the eurozone under new rules aimed at reducing budget deficits and public debt. These powers intrude deeply into national sovereignty because the Commission analyses countries' draft national budgets <u>before national parliaments debate them</u>, and can ask for revisions. The Commission then makes recommendations and its proposed sanctions can only be stopped if a qualified majority in the Council of Ministers votes against them."** *(Heather Grabbe).* In other words, the EU now has the power to stop an elected government's budget. Democracy is now at an end, in Europe. We are the children and the rulers are our unelected parents.

You must obey European Union laws -
- however undemocratically they are made.

The laws made by the European Union are legally binding and you must obey them. You will notice it as more and more, EU laws override our own laws. We are used to taking it for granted that we are governed only by our Parliament, and have only to obey British law, which we have developed ourselves and which we have some control over. But that is no longer the case. European law, made by a handful of appointed Commissioners, takes precedence over British law.

Democrats in France and other countries protest as we do, but that is the fact of life in the European Union.

This dreadful project relies upon the ignorance of 100s of millions of people. The complicatedness, the similar sounding names for all the functions and bodies, the Councils and Committees and Commissions, all contribute to a certain power that lies in unknowability. The overall impression is one of a frustrating but vague bureaucratic body. However that impression conceals a far more sinister truth; the replacement of democratic government by an unelected and unremovable bureaucratic administrative dictatorship.

Unless you feel confident that you are influencing the laws being made in Europe when you vote in a Euro-election, you should think about what power is being wielded over you.

Who, if anyone, has the right to give away British Sovereignty?

The British Parliament has hidden this outrage against democracy by routinely making EU directives into British law. The signing of successive treaties which have piecemeal given away British sovereignty is a betrayal of trust. We have not elected our MPs to give away British sovereignty, and in fact they have no legal right to do so. Technically they are probably guilty of treason, and the Queen's signature on the Acts means that she too is a party to the giving away of sovereignty to foreign powers. These sorts of questions about the legality of what is being done are not taken seriously, at present. What is being done is passively accepted. That doesn't mean that, at some point, the law won't be brought to bear upon the question, if and when we wake up to realise what is happening. But in the meantime, we need to address the question very quickly about who, if anyone, has the right to actually give away sovereignty, before any further moves are made.

Even aside from the EU's gross failings in elementary democracy, the sheer scale of the European Union works very much against the chance of there being effective control of the executive by the people. There are 450 million people in the European Union. That fact alone makes the proper functioning of democracy problematic. The fact that those 450 million people are from entirely different countries with completely different histories and internal developments, different outlooks on life, ways of life, philosophies, beliefs and religions, as well as being at different stages of economic and even social and political development, adds to the difficulty. If there were no choice but to have one rubber stamp parliament for 450 million people with only 700 seats, (that's one seat for every 640,000 people; in our democracy it's one seat for every 99,000 people) and to have an endless series of diktats made by 27 appointees, if this were imposed upon us by force, then it would seem a dreadful fate. But to voluntarily place ourselves in that situation is perverse, and we cannot simply presume that it will not lead to a very substantial loss of freedom, or worse.

The setting up of the EU without plebiscites also goes against the *Self Determination* principle which is at the very foundation of the United Nations. The right of a nation to self determination has been one the guiding principles of international law since the League of Nations was formed in 1919. The forced change of nationhood that the gradual formation of the EU into a state to replace the 27 nation states involves, is in contravention of Article 15 of the Universal Declaration of Human Rights, which states; *everyone has the right to a nationality and that no one should be arbitrarily deprived of a nationality*. The persistent refusal to hold referendums in the member states of the EU is a serious violation of this basic principle, which has been written into international law as a human right. Despite the seriousness of the denial of such a right to millions of people, the demands for a referendum in Britain are deftly handled by deflection as if it were a mere political game, which can be won by delay and postponement - until it is too late. If a government were to refuse a referendum on the removal of basic democratic rights in any other circumstances, there would be an uprising, even in Britain. There isn't, simply because people don't know what the EU actually is.

Politics depends very much on a local connection to power. It depends on the possibility of changing things. Even now we feel insufficiently powerful to effect change through voting, that is why there is such a low turn out at elections. That is also, paradoxically, why we seem prepared to give away our democratic rights. But in a European constituency of 450 million people, the chance of influencing politics, of bringing about change, shrinks drastically, once power has been made so immense and to cover such a large area.

Already the sheer scale and complexity of the European Union and our involvement in it is being used as a reason why we cannot leave it. What does that tell you about how responsive a democracy it is?

Fruitcakes and racists

Words like "racist" are being used to silence opinion in areas that not related to it, to make people afraid to talk about immigration from Europe. We do however have to face the taboo and have the debate.

It is hard to write about this aspect without mentioning how the media, in concert with the main parties, has connived to discredit anti-EU opinion, notably the UK Independence Party. That party has been characterised as particularly odd ball and untrustworthy, full of strange extremists. I don't claim to have very extensive knowledge of the membership of that party, or of the other parties, but the truth is most likely that there are easily as many oddball extremists to be found in the other parties' ranks. It is to the shame of the Conservative Party that they resorted to smears when they noticed that their own support was drifting in the local elections. In the end the electorate duly punished them. But it should be noted that a British Prime Minister said this of a centrist party; "UKIP is sort of a bunch of...fruitcakes and loonies and closet racists mostly". Most Labour supporters have allowed themselves to be told the same sort of thing and believe it. It is frightening that what is after all surely a mainstream middle of the road party formed around a body of opinion wanting to preserve our democratic rights, has been so successfully characterised as "extremist". The most disturbing story has to be that concerning the parents who had their foster children taken away from them by a Labour council on the grounds that "they belonged to a racist party" because they were members of UKIP. This was based on the fact that UKIP had said things about "multiculturalism", which is nothing to do with racism (In France, for example it is the left who see multiculturalism as a threat to the Equality that is one of the principles of the Republic). The significant aspect is that the main parties try to block normal political discussion of such an important issue as the future of our democracy; Both Labour and Conservative try to render central aspects of the discussion taboo. What is also significant is that these attempts were punished at the ballot box, shortly afterwards. We might wonder how powerful such proscriptive behaviour and such connivance would be, if there were no power of the electorate to counter it. And that is the very situation we face in the near future, as part of the EU where policy makers do not have to refer to the electorate.

Stop press!!!

Just as I was writing this and about to send it to the printer, lo and behold the German and French governments did a u-turn on immigration in the EU. On the eve of the lifting of restrictions on Romanians and Croatians and Bulgarians, the Socialist French President, M. Hollande, declared that unlimited immigration would "destroy the fabric of France". And the German coalition government seemed to agree with him and called for limits to immigration.

Effectively this means that they do not actually believe in the 4 pillars of the EU, especially not the free movement of peoples.

Meanwhile the Hungarian Commissioner called Britain "the nasty county of Europe" for expressing the very same concerns as the French and the Germans.

So maybe next time when working class people express *their* concerns, the Europhiles and the middle class left can remember that the Socialists in France are also xenophobes and racists, and the new Germans, in fact the architects of the EU found that they didn't quite like the effects of it as much as they thought they would.

And when it suddenly dawns on them what the real consequences of open borders are, as it seems to have done, maybe they can all look back at the scorn, derision and contempt they have poured on the working class people who have expressed concerns about the effect on their standard of living and their jobs.

Of course there is room for thinking that we would like to help people in poorer countries than our own, although we might want to help the starving first, rather than the less well off in Europe. Governments offer to limit non-EU immigration thinking it is a sop to public concerns about EU immigration. Surely that is a racist distinction at the heart of the EU immigration policy? Isn't the open EU internal borders policy is by extension built on a *closed EU external borders* policy? Dont we in Britain have a first duty to accept economic migrants from former colonies, rather than Europeans?

But if we decide, after open debate with no taboos, that helping poor Europeans is something we would like to do, as a priority, then we should be clear about what it would mean, if we do it by opening our borders to the EU. It would mean a significant drop in the standard of living in Britain (and any other wealthy country that wanted to do it). It would mean levelling out the standard of living, averaging it out, to somewhere between the Romanian standard and our own. But let us be clear that it should not be only the people at the bottom of our own society who should pay the price. It should be rather the richest who should pay first. The fairest and clearest way to start sharing out the wealth to the unlimited immigrants from poorer European countries would be to tax the rich 90% on everything they earn over £50,000. They would still be richer than everyone else, but we can imagine how much they would like it. We would see then just how much they really wanted immigration when it was driving *their* income down.   Would they then be racists for not wanting it?

BBC executives for example who get £186,000 would then get £63,00 instead, the rest would go to paying the unemployment benefit and housing benefit, and council tax benefit and health care for the poor Romanians who we would be glad to welcome here, to live in Hampstead and Highgate, and Holland Park....

But then, if we are going to share, and it seems that the middle classes do want to share, then why are we only going to share with the *new* poor who come? Why not share with the old poor who are already here (many of them are immigrants too). The whole idea in fact is maybe a revelation, it might be a catalyst to more sharing in our society.

Meanwhile young doctors from the poorer countries of Europe are leaving to come to the richer countries, where they are paid 8 times the salaries they could earn at home. This leaves their own health services bereft of doctors.

"Bulgaria has the lowest wages in the EU and doctors' salaries are no exception. Dr Balezdrov earns around £800 a month (950 Euros;). If he worked in the same field in the UK, he would earn £60-70,000 a year. "(BBC 20th November 2013).

What is next?

Economic policy and all laws concerning trade, right down to how you weigh your vegetables or measure cloth or wood, are now largely decided by the EU Commission (with punishments attached for disobedience). Federalists, who are the driving force behind Europe, have the ambition to extend European law into more areas, and to unify European law. Already the Commission has been given new powers to control and sanction, and therefore over-rule, national budgets made by elected governments. It is a long slow relentless drive, that can never be defeated, only slowed down.

What if the EU was to become democratic?

What if there is a sudden change, what if against all the odds the EU does really become democratic, so that its government is actually formed by the opinion of the 450 million disparate peoples of Europe? What would that be like? Would it be a good thing to be a part of the huge multinational EU, even in those circumstances? It will be European opinion, *if any*, that will determine our laws, not British opinion. Do you feel we have the same needs from criminal law as Poles, Romanians and Germans? Is one law to suit all countries the best way to get good laws?

And how would the party system work then? How would the voting blocs work in the European parliament (*if* the parliament was to form the government). If loyalties and alliances were formed along the current lines, would then for example the socialist MEPs of Romania vote alongside the Labour MEPs from Britain; the conservative MEPs from Lithuania vote alongside the conservatives from Sweden or Denmark, and the outcome, the government of Europe, would that be formed by those alliances? In what way would those very different forms of conservatism and socialism be determining the kind of government they wanted by voting together? And what if they didn't vote together, for that very reason? What chance would voters in Britain or Romania have of being able to know about, predict, or understand the actual outcome of elections, across such a diverse and contradictory constituency, where the parties and groupings have misleading names? In what way would such an electorate be enjoying real self determination? Would the outcome of such an election reflect the intentions of the voters? People complain already, in our own comparatively homogeneous nation, of frustration at feeling powerless to effect politics. Making the electorate 7 times bigger and 27 times more disparate is not likely the way to create a responsive democracy. If it feels pointless to vote now, imagine what it would feel like to vote for a government of Europe? One thing is for certain, if the EU does ever become a real democracy, then Westminster will disappear. Feel the law should be changed? Want to protest about your local hospital closure? Then write to your *Euro* MP, and see if he can change the course of a state of 450 million people.

And concerning the location of political power; A reminder...

It may seem odd or it may seem obvious, but one important but unspoken part of the invisible contract which supports democracy, is the physical relationship between ourselves and those who rule in our name. In Britain we have never had a large standing army. Our small army could never hope to contain the people if the consensus that allows the government to have power over us ever broke down. This is a very good safeguard of our freedoms. If they go too far, if they refuse to have an election, we know where they are and we can go and remove them by force.

But imagine 20 years from now, when the European Union has extended its undemocratic legislative powers into all areas of life, criminal law, the police, domestic taxation, immigration, and all domestic laws. Imagine if we decide that we would prefer, after all, not to obey the dictatorship? Where will we go to lay hands on the government that will control us then? To Brussels? To Strasbourg?

Or maybe we will soon face the water cannons of EuroPolice on the streets of London? In the 1960s 200 Algerian demonstrators "disappeared" by the banks of the Seine, and reappeared as corpses in the river. Don't like the British Police? Try the European ones.

THE IMPORTANT THING ABOUT GOVERNMENTS IS THAT YOU NEED TO KEEP THEM WHERE YOU CAN GET AT THEM.

But wait, is the European Union good for trade?

What did Gordon Brown, the last great Labour Chancellor think.....?

"No business planning for growth in the future can ignore the facts: 80% of our potential markets are outside Europe and a decade from now the Asian market will be 50% larger than the European." *(Gordon Brown).*

So...is Europe really worth giving away our democracy for?

The European Community is an economic trading organisation with an undefined political aspect which is by turns insisted upon and denied by ministers. This is acknowledged by **Gordon Brown** who described the intentions behind the EU; **"Indeed the assumptions that became rooted in the very idea of European integration were that the single market and single currency would lead to tax harmonisation, a federal fiscal policy and something akin to a federal state".**

While it is reasonable to belong to a trading block, it is not reasonable to give away political power to do so. Remember that political power means the power to decide over our lives.

Do we need to swap democracy for trade in Europe?

So imperious are the economic imperatives, that opponents of the European Community are painted as being hopelessly petty and deluded, pathetic flag wavers failing to see the bigger picture of what the markets tell us; even though, in actual fact, the markets tell us to look beyond Europe, as we always have done.

The benefits of a Europe-wide trading block are no doubt great. Napoleon and Hitler offered us the same perks although with rather more obvious political disadvantages, but again a certain loss of political power. We felt at that time quite able to decline, despite the considerable inconvenience involved for everyone.

The same benefits are offered now by our friends, and are naturally harder to resist. Britain, like any country has an appetite and a need for trade with its neighbours, and we naturally delight in the peace that now reigns in Europe. But we do not need to give away democracy in exchange for peace in Europe. And that peace in Europe was not achieved by abandoning democracy - was it? No, it was achieved by upholding democracy. Last time democracy was swept away in Europe there were very serious consequences for hundreds of millions of people. The loss of democracy even continued for decades after the defeat of fascism, as millions of Europeans had to live in the Eastern bloc, another economic dictatorship. Many Europeans are sadly used to living without democracy. We need to think very carefully before allowing that to happen again.

The greatest advantage to Britain in the trading block with Europe is not trade within Europe, but that it better protects our interests vis à vis the USA, and the Eastern countries. But Gordon Brown himself has said that the endless EU rules and regulations hinder rather than help our trade chances with the rest of the world. There is no need to give away political power for that.

Britain's trade historically has been with the rest of the world; it is there that we have our longest and closest links. For a brief period, three decades, it seemed as if we were about to pursue a new destiny in Europe, and this meant not only trade links, it meant, according to the architects of the European Community, political and cultural convergence. Already their vision is seen to be out of date; rejected by electorates around Europe who share, actually, the British distrust of a federal vision, the narrower picture of Europe trading with itself, dominated by its own internal rules, and with its sovereignties constricted by tax 'harmonisation'.

This inward looking aspect of the European Community, and the way in which it is increasingly overwhelmed by a flood of rules and restrictions and bureaucracy (despite its recent rather desperate but telling, "bonfire" of regulations) actually threaten trade with the East.

This is how Gordon Brown put it;

"...moving from the trade bloc era to the era of Global Europe requires a long term commitment to *regulatory reform* that balances the need to lessen the burden of regulation and enhance our flexibility while still ensuring high standards.

In Britain I am determined that we not only impose a competitiveness test to all new regulations but pioneer a risk based approach to regulation.

"It is globalisation that is our greatest future challenge: world trade doubling every decade, China's trade doubling every three years, world trade now rising nearly twice as fast as world output. Two decades ago just 10 per cent of manufacturing exports came from developing countries. Soon it will be 50%. China's wage costs are still just 5 per cent of those of the European Union. But we are not simply competing in low skilled, low wage mass production manufacturing. With 4 million graduates a year from China's and India's universities, we are now competing with Asia on high tech, high skilled, high

value added goods too. And so no country or continent, however successful today, can take its long term prosperity for granted."

... and in case there is any doubt left about how useful to Britain's global trading the EU is;

"...in the move from trade bloc Europe to Global Europe, old policies will not be just out of date but counter productive for the global era."

This is how the Labour Chancellor saw the future for Europe;

"...the question for us is how Europe can move from the older inward-looking model to a flexible, reforming, open and globally-oriented Europe - able to master the economic challenge from Asia, America and beyond."

This has to invite the question; Is it worth being in it at all?

It is clear that Gordon Brown had a very different view of what is necessary than the rest of the EU leaders. But because we are part of the EU we are not free to follow our own judgement, but have to obey European directives, no matter how damaging to our economic prosperity.

Is *leaving* the EU a threat to trade?

Britain is the third biggest market in Europe. Leaving the EU does not threaten British trade as we buy more from European countries than they do from us - in other words - they need our trade more than we need theirs - trade will continue. It would not be in the EU's interest to erect trade barriers (as some people fear they would do if we left, and there is no need for us to do it either). When Gordon Brown was Chancellor he complained of EU regulations already hindering British industry. There is no reason not to have friendly trade agreements with European neighbours or partners, just as non EU countries still have. And as more countries allow their electorates to speak, more countries will follow suit.

Do we have to leave? Can't we reform it from the inside?

One of the main features of the EU, that makes it so undesirable, is its enormous and unwieldy nature. It's own constitution, expressed deceitfully in treaties, is deliberately impenetrable, while the sheer size of the bureaucracy acts as a protective shield against comprehension, let alone reform. Even if it were the most democratic body in the world, which it is not, it is in fact one of the least democratic, it would still be difficult for the will of the people to be effectively expressed across such a vast constituency. To reform, to direct, to change, to influence such a vast organisation is not just difficult but in fact contrary to its design and purpose. The EU is conceived as a bulwark against the will of the people, which is seen as prey to mistakes and demagoguery. The EU is set up by administrative bureaucrats *for* administrative bureaucrats, and is hostile to democratic expression. That hostility is built into its institutions. Maybe in 100 years time, after many trials and upheavals, it may turn into a democracy, but it isn't one now. We already have one, at Westminster where, for all its shortcomings, the will of the people can be expressed and heard,

Only people who think that the status quo is satisfactory should want to surrender our political rights to an unelected EU government, that pays no heed to an electorate.

If anyone on the left for example thinks that something remains to be won, such as equality of wealth, pay, housing conditions, in Britain, then they had better make sure that we preserve democracy.

It is to say the very least, unwise to give away democratic power in fair weather that cannot be easily regained in foul. Our parliament is where the British people express their political will. With each bit of power that is taken away from Westminster and put in Europe, we must ask ourselves 1) if we can afford to lose that power? and 2) how would we ever get it back again.

Does it make good sense to allow a new upper class of political elites, outside the reach of democracy, to rule us from abroad?

While you read this you are possibly thinking "Yes, but its not literally true". But it is. European laws have to be obeyed, and they are made in all areas except, so far, criminal law, immigration (which is anyway determined by European law), and taxation (except that national budgets are now going to be subject to the Commissioner's approval before Parliament even sees them). And we have seen how the European so-called Human Rights laws interfere in British judicial decisions. And when we are completely subject to

European law in all areas of the legal system, how long will it be then until there will be talk of scaling down the British Parliament, as it will gradually become obsolete? 30 years? 20 years? 15 years? How long have we got?

How long will it be before people are led by the press into thinking that Westminster is an unnecessary expense as it no longer makes the laws?

People are used to presuming, without justification, that European human rights laws, for example, are more liberal than our own. Well, if they are, which they are not, what happens when they aren't? What will you be able to do about it? Will you go on a protest march in Trafalgar Square? Will your EU masters be bothered by that? Do people realise that EU laws can be used to over-ride trade union collective bargaining, as they already have been in Sweden and Luxembourg and Finland, and Germany; and that they are framed to do just that?

Are you complacent about handing over power to the European Union?

Do you trust it will be ok? Do you think the sound of the EU is more forward-looking than our old fashioned democracy? Do you perhaps not know or bother to find out, how it works? Do you maybe not know how our own system works? Do you think 'they're all more or less the same'? Do you think all politicians are "corrupt" so it doesn't matter anyway?

A Working Class Alternative To Labour

What happens when EU laws are *not* the kind you want?
When they are *not* liberal, or socialist or social democrat or
whatever it is you want them to be? It is staggeringly naive to
simply trust a regime to be "nice" because you have the vague
impression that they are, based largely on them seeming to be
more "modern" or progressive than our democratically
elected representatives. And when you notice that they are
doing precisely what they want with no reference to any sort
of political influence from the people, what then will you do?
What happens when you realise they form governments
without even mentioning to the electorate of Europe what
their policies are going to be? How then will you fight for
higher wages, for better schools or hospitals, or for the rights
of minorities, or for control of the police force, or for the
kind of laws you want there to be? You might dislike the
government our democracy has served you up with this time,
but at least you know who they are, you know their names,
you know their policies; and they have to justify those
policies before a vigorous opposition all day every day in
Parliament, and you know that eventually their popularity
will wane and you and people who think like you, will be able
to get rid of them in an election. You know that after that
government has lost the election, they have to go, not the
following week, or the following month or the following year,
or never, but the following morning. Out! Gone! Door
slammed after them. Now whatever jejune, infantile remarks
we can make about how "this lot is the same as the last lot,
they're all the same as each other," etc, the fact is - it's not
true in our system. And in some systems it is. Literally.
Literally the same people are in power from one government

to the next. We need to be very careful before we allow our "healthy cynicism " about our own system to allow us to talk ourselves into something a lot worse. A people that willingly allows its democratically elected representatives to be replaced by appointed ones - deserve to get a shock. And if we do it we will get one.

The fact that most people still do not know how the EU works ought to ring alarm bells. It is most unfortunate that ignorance and complacency about our *own* political system have reached such depths, just at a time when we are in danger of giving power away to an essentially non-democratic organisation. It is more important than ever to teach about our Parliament in schools, before we have bred a generation who will know so little of its value that they will give it away.

It is perhaps partly because the working classes have felt so long they have no party to represent their interests in Parliament, and that material equality is an ever-receding goal, that cynicism about Westminster is at its height. That is a very dangerous thing. For however useless our own parliament may seem to the low paid, they can expect little mercy from an unelected dictatorship of bureaucrats whose aim is to provide cheap labour. Better the devil you can hang from the lamp-posts in Westminster than the devil you cannot get to and cannot remove by either election or insurrection.

Any working class government, in the interests of preserving democracy for the British people, ought to hold a referendum on EU membership *immediately it was elected.*

*

132

Housing and Poverty

Housing - the great indicator of social inequality

Where you live is surely one of the most important aspects of poverty. The middle classes know about this, they always make sure they live in exactly the right place. We take it for granted that certain areas or types of area are accompanied by certain types of serious social problem. And social problems mean personal problems facing families and individuals which limit and determine their whole lives. In a country with the kind of inequality we have in Britain, being born into certain types of areas and circumstances can pretty much determine what kind of life you are likely to get, including health. So much do we take it for granted, and so much do we accept it as inevitable, that we perhaps do not ask; *Why should millions of people live in worse conditions than the rest of us?*

"A million children live in substandard housing and half a million live in overcrowded housing." *(Social Care Institute for Excellence)*. And of course the phrase 'substandard housing' has nothing to do with the nature of the *surroundings*. How many more millions of people live in areas that lessen their chances of a good life? It is a malaise in Britain that is so widespread it's hard to quantify.

Is it possible to live in a society without those kinds of areas, without lives that are blighted before they have even begun?

Is it *necessary* that whole communities are ridden with poverty, unemployment, crime, violence, abuse, ill-health and bad education?

Is it *acceptable,* to our society as a whole that large numbers of people are born into and grow up in, communities with these problems?

Is it *wise* to allow it, considering the consequences for society as a whole?

The word *modern* is often used very loosely in various contexts, including politics, usually to justify change that cannot be justified in any more substantial way. But we rarely hear whether it is consistent with *modern* ideals that this ancient practise of consigning a large proportion of the population to lifetimes of misery be allowed to persist, with no real effort to finally stop it. The welfare state was a step along the way, but it remains more a means of alleviating poverty than of actually eradicating it. So does the Living Wage Campaign. The step towards equality has not been taken.

Not Accepting Inequality

Poverty and inequality hold back our society from development. It is even evident in the gradual degradation of our cultural life. Dumbing down isn't just about finding the lowest common denominator in education or broadcasting for example, it is about the better-off themselves being undermined by the falsehood of their own position which weakens the whole body of society. The infantilism and fake sentimentality which pervades the press and media is partly a consequence of living a lie. This lie applies especially to middle class Labour voters, as they profess to have egalitarian principles, but have no visible objections to the vast inequalities between their incomes and those of the low paid. They went out onto the streets to protest about student fees, when the government's student loans changes did not adversely affect the low paid (I know they didn't from recent personal experience). The new arrangements *do* adversely affect the better-off, they now have to pay more of their children's expenses in further education. And why shouldn't they? But they were out protesting, led there by the left wing press who told them it was a draconian measure against the poor. The press even said, later, that even if the measures themselves didn't mean that those on low incomes had to pay until they were earning a middle class salary, they put poor people off going to university because they *thought* they had to pay. This despite it being the newspapers themselves who deliberately gave this false impression. And so the left wing middle classes went boldly out onto the streets to protest - the public school educated son of the public school educated David Gilmour of Pink Floyd ("We don't need no education") cavorted on the memorial to the war dead to register his disgust at his rich (worth £78m) parents having to pay his Cambridge University fees. You couldn't make it up. That is what left wing protest has become in this country. But when did the left wing middle classes go out in force to demonstrate against poverty pay for the working classes? Never.

It is significant that those who protested against the student fees, thought they were acting in a left wing cause. Yet it was a moderate measure, aimed at the better off, which didn't affect the low paid and which brought Britain into line with more socialist countries such as Sweden. And yet because it was carried out by a Conservative government, albeit in coalition, it could be presented as draconian. If we have lost the ability to evaluate fairly without prejudice in politics, that is a bad thing indeed. If the left wing cause has so closely been associated with middle class interest, then we need a new working class impetus.

It will perhaps one day be the work of a civilised society, a turning point in the future, to decide that we are no longer willing to accept that large numbers of our fellow citizens have markedly inferior lives to the rest of us. Will we grow into a society that isn't prepared to stand by and allow the misery of millions of its citizens? Will we one day insist that we all have the same right to a decent life? Will we ever be a society that is not willing to be humiliated by the spectacle of its own selfishness? A more mature society that takes care of all its members?

What is to be done?

What we are talking about when we mention poverty and housing, is the effects of poverty, concentrated in place and by time; Poor areas and housing estates often have many families who have been poor for more than one or two generations, and the effects upon these are cumulative. The modern society deals with this problem by small piecemeal means, by detailed and painstaking work. Social services and governments think in terms of problem families; social workers do it because they have to, governments do it because it is a way of using the limited resources, both material and intellectual and moral, allocated to deal with the problem. In other words, talking in terms of problem families distracts from the wider and more obvious causes of the problem which we are so far unwilling to deal with, inequality.

Raising the minimum wage of the employed to £9.30 is not on its own going to solve the problem of long term poverty and of the effect of poor areas.

Raising benefit levels to 20% below these for the unemployed is not on its own going to solve the problem either.

Returning to industrial production so that we are engaged in making what we use and paying our way as a nation and as individuals, won't even solve the problem of poor areas on its own.

Making schools suitable and able to educate people for the jobs and lives they are going to have, and making grammar schools available to everyone who wants one, won't on its own free our country from the existence of areas of poverty and misery.

Breaking the grip of the youth gangs by the vigorous and relentless daily action of a beat police force that is part of, and controlled by, the community they operate in, is not on its own the solution to the violence and fear which reigns over many working class areas in our cities.

Even creating an egalitarian and prosperous society of shared and equal responsibility and opportunity (including wages) won't stop certain areas being concentrated in misery.

That won't stop until housing policy and the market players which are the builders and developers, acknowledge that everyone has the same right to a decent sized and pleasantly presented and situated home. There are more egalitarian societies than our own, in Europe, which still have managed to create what are in effect slums, where the design and appearance and scale of mass housing manages to overcome the good effects of decent wages to anyway create the hard and inhuman qualities of slum buildings which so adversely affect the young people growing up in them. This is because these places express in their very natures the unstated contempt for the people destined to live their lives in them, just as low wages express contempt for the people forced to accept them.

The problem of housing cannot be separated from the problems of class and inequality in our society.

In other words, there is a huge problem facing our society; namely that there are millions of badly designed, overcrowded, substandard, ugly, inhuman habitations, for the working classes to live in, designed by middle class architects who live in detached Georgian houses. Millions of our housing stock, most of it very modern, are not really fit for happy human habitation.

Whether it is housing associations or councils or developers who build "affordable homes", the principle of equal rights, or expectations that should be met, in housing, is one that has yet to be established. Taking gross inequalities in housing for granted is perhaps an attitude of the class society that is most difficult to shake off.

A society committed to equality of material and mental well-being would have to face the responsibility and the challenge to its imagination and creative ability, to as quickly as possible replace this housing with homes large enough and attractive enough for...MIDDLE CLASS people to live in. Because most housing where working class people are expected to live is not. And we as a society accept that should naturally be the case. That is in itself one of the greatest pieces of evidence that our society is one based on presumptions of class and inequality. A working class government ought to reject those presumptions. It is time that working class housing was as spacious and attractive as middle class housing.

When that is achieved, and when all the other causes of poverty are removed, then there will be no more working class slums than there are middle class ones.

Homelessness

There are roughly 50,000 homeless families, insofar as they have no permanent housing. It would cost approximately £3 billion to house them. Remember it is the economic system, which we are told works automatically to provide for demand, that has failed to provide sufficient homes for the

139

demand. It does this by ignoring demand that is not expressed by a desire or ability to borrow £250,000 from a bank, even though homes cost far less than that to build. In reality of course, demand for housing comes from those needing and wanting a home.

There are approximately 1800 people sleeping rough in Britain each night, and it would cost approximately £15m each year to house them.

These are pressing costs, which need to be met, and have to be met, and should be met, by the rest of us to prevent the shameful situation of homelessness in a society where property and homes are for so many a source of huge profits, one of the inequalities which undermine our society.

A working class government should as a priority make a spending commitment to the building, or funding through housing associations, of affordable (but not substandard in size or design) homes to meet the full demand. A tax (the only use of extra, rather than redistributed, tax mentioned in this book) on new-builds of homes *over a certain market value* would help to fund it, and also make affordable housing a priority in the building industry.

This situation also illustrates how *expensive* poverty is. A society which chooses to maintain poverty by keeping successive generations on low wages, and by failing to maintain its industrial base thus condemning millions to permanent unemployment, is bound to give itself an expensive homelessness problem in the long run. It is an unavoidable consequence of poverty, because when people are poor they cannot always successfully provide for themselves or their children. Obviously.

A society which eradicates low pay and which creates full employment by manufacturing what it uses, will make a step towards eradicating homelessness.

Council housing, immigration, unemployment and low wages.

In recent years Labour politicians such as Frank Field have acknowledged that the working classes have a right to object to immigrants being given priority for council housing, without being called racists. It is perhaps because they are so well off that the middle classes who now dominate the Labour Party can't imagine anyone actually *needing* a council house.

Middle class Labourites have great difficulty allowing the working classes to have any opinions about how their own areas develop, and about their chances of getting council homes, and despise the working classes for views they have decided are racist.

The British working classes are not typically racists. Firstly many of them are immigrants themselves, and it is the working classes who live and work with new waves of immigrants, and share their areas and communities with them. One might wonder how the middle classes would react if their areas and their communities, forms of entertainment etc. were transformed by high levels of immigration. Well, we know what they do. They move away. The working classes need no lessons about racism from the middle classes, whose idea of absorbing immigration often amounts to no more than giving other people's council homes away, and enjoying foreign restaurants.

The other subject upon which the working classes have been silenced is immigration and unemployment. When working class people have complained that immigrants are taking their jobs they are called racists (even though, again, they may be immigrants themselves). In fact the perception is broadly correct. Cheap foreign labour has been used to push down working class wages.

Yet despite this the British working classes harbour no specific resentment against those workers themselves. While there is indeed racism in British society, Britain (and we are talking about working class areas) is a comparatively tolerant society, where large numbers of immigrants are able to settle and to maintain their own identities, as well as to integrate. And despite there being no active party to express working class views and concerns, and despite understandable anger about not being listened to about the destiny of their communities, the British working classes give less support to the far right than those parties receive in almost any other country in Europe.

A working class party should be based on solidarity between workers regardless of course of their race or origins. Putting an end to the practice of using successive waves of immigrants to push down the wages of the previous wave, is naturally a part of any working class party policy. Immigrants coming to Britain, not just from the EU but from areas where immigrants have traditionally come from to Britain, when there is a proper material equality, will not be driving wages down, and they will not be living in ghettos or in poverty.

A society that vigorously protects the vulnerable

There is often an institutionalised reluctance to act in defence of victims of crime. We suffer from moral cowardice and take refuge in sentimental fantasies about wrongdoers rather than face the unpleasant facts about the suffering of vulnerable people. Britain needs to develop its sense of solidarity and community to ensure that the vulnerable are effectively protected. This means greater police powers to intervene directly and promptly against bullying, racism, aggression, and nuisance, on estates or on the streets or in schools; or it can also mean protecting the poor against loan companies.

Too often we have heard how vulnerable people have been subjected to years of abuse and the police and councils have failed to protect them actively. Beat policing, which *literally* means police regularly patrolling a beat on foot, would be a useful measure against so called 'low level' crime, that sometimes means life and death to its victims. This has already been partially re-introduced in the form of Community Police, and needs to be extended. The regular police force too should return to the beat. Needless to say, the police need to be finally and conclusively rescued from the current neurotic preoccupation with bureaucracy so that they can do the job they are paid for. In this case as in many others, bureaucracy signifies more than a waste of time and money. It expresses the outlook on life of the class whose invention it is. Our society would do well to move actively away from it. Its philosophy needs to be called into question.

143

"Bullying is not a word we use here"

Bullying in schools has had a lot of attention, and the result has been that quite often schools have an anti-bullying policy. That policy sometimes revolves around some strange contorted posturing on the part of the school, "Bullying is not a word we use here", where the official policy against bullying is to pretend, to insist, it doesn't happen. The other contortion is to pretend that the victim of bullying is somehow complicit and partly if not completely to blame, an extension of the "shake hands and make up" school of thought. These curious misfunctions of previous attempts to address the widespread problem, are indications that our society lacks even the moral courage to deal with badly behaved children, even when it comes to defending the extremely vulnerable. Further evidence of that can be seen on the streets. Teachers need to know that bullying can ruin lives; there is surely enough evidence of it to satisfy any sceptic on that point. It needs to be made a clear responsibility of all schools to stop it happening. "Having a policy" is not the same thing. We need to ensure, in this as in many other matters, that bureaucratic measures, lip service and box ticking, don't replace real human moral responsibility and activity. It is perhaps a shame that natural instincts and common sense have been scared away from many aspects of social life, by the bureaucratic machine left on autopilot. It would perhaps be one benefit of a greater working class influence upon our society, if that effect were to be reduced.

The poor are still preyed upon by firms offering payday loans of up to 5000%. After decades of this, which was ignored by Labour and Tory governments alike, there has recently been talk of capping the loan rate. We need to set a legal limit to the interest on loans at, for example, 15% per year, and to abolish the power of bailiffs except those enforcing Magistrates Court penalties, and outlaw home visits to collect debts (legally this is already the position but the practise continues and should be actively prosecuted).

A loan rate cap wouldn't just affect the payday loan companies which would be thereby made illegal, but also the activities of banks and other credit agencies, including credit cards. This kind of interference in the free market is anathema to governments because it seems to represent the crossing of an invisible line. It is fairly obvious why, since it would be part of a programme to spread profit downwards, away from those who already own capital.

Fines imposed by local authorities and the courts should be calculated by daily earnings to ensure the same proportion of punishment for rich and poor. The courts generally take earnings into account, but fixed fines set by councils don't. That is an unacceptable burden upon the low paid, and it is unjust.

Eg. A fine, say for parking or speeding, could be set at a quarter of a day's pay; so the amount would vary according to the individual's salary. A man on the proposed minimum wage of £19.400 pa would pay a fine of £13, another man on £180,000 pa would pay £123. The deterrent aspect would be the same for both.

Parking charges and other motoring fines in Britain, are a national disgrace. These fines and charges in particular represent a hidden tax on the poor, since because they are at a flat rate they affect people on low incomes disproportionately. The swingeingly high flat rate parking and motoring offence fines and their often unreasonable enforcement by greedy Local Councils has made motoring increasingly a preserve of the rich, especially in London. Meanwhile the use of cameras, sometimes mounted on circulating spy cars, are such a disproportionate use of state power against the people, that they ought to raise serious questions about civil liberties. It is hard not to see the overbearing and, for the poor, frightening use of techniques of enforcement, as a sort of dress rehearsal for a broader state/local council tyranny. Action must be taken specifically to halt it. The situation certainly creates bad habits of power wielding in local government, and of passivity before mindless legislation on the part of the people, who are systematically crushed into submission by local governments' engines of oppression. Normal people are terrified to risk a car journey in-case they fall foul of the unfair system weighted against the low paid.

It is part of any egalitarian society, that the less well off should not be punished more than the wealthy. Flat rate fines in a society with huge inequalities of income like ours, are especially unfair. The reason it has been allowed to continue for so long, and has received so little attention in the press, is precisely that journalists generally belong to the class of earner for whom a parking fine is nothing more than an inconvenience. For the low paid it is a catastrophe.

A national 2hr free parking scheme (already operational in some towns and in other countries), would remove most parking charges. Councils should be obliged to provide sufficient parking spaces to serve small shops, essential for all communities. This is vital if small retailers are to survive.

Local government parking policies, along with business rates, are well known to have eventually fatal consequences for small shops on high streets, and yet, despite its palpable and visible effects on our society, the problem gets no attention from national politicians. It is a bewildering sight to see small local shops actively persecuted by council parking "services" when these shops are already struggling for survival against the megastores, whose receipt of generous planning and other permissions from councils can only be put down to the size of their wallets. Councils are generally seen to serve the interests of the great against the small.

The parking scandal, in which locally elected representatives behave like feudal overlords, one of the biggest frauds perpetrated upon the people, is indicative of the general corruption and arrogance of local government. The government simplified some of the rules surrounding probity in 2011, (Localism Act 2011) precisely because of the widespread problems, but it doesn't seem to have made a difference, at least not to public trust in local government.

The Committee for Standards in Public Life has reported on the government's Localism Act 2011, and found that "the lack of available sanctions and independent scrutiny risked damaging public confidence in the probity of local government."

Local government has considerable power. When it takes that power illegally it is still up to individuals to go to court to prevent them; when councils, for example, illegally raise revenue by the imposition of parking schemes. In a recent case in 2012 Barnet Council was found guilty by the High Court of doing just that, of using parking as a means to tax the poor. The case had to be brought by an individual.

Local governments take liberties with the people that national government would baulk at. Many feel there is a culture of bribery and corruption at local government level, especially involving planning and contracts, and council employment. However, the widespread public distrust of local government combined with passive tolerance of it is symptomatic of a more general failing of local democracy. Public cynicism is a result of public powerlessness, and ignorance of our own systems of government.

The level and quality of political campaigning in local elections is often pitifully low, lacking in detail and honesty, relying on little more than a few slogans. Local elections ought to more accurately reflect the power wielded by local government.

The power of bureaucracy to preserve inequality

People of all classes are growing used to being powerless in the face of bureaucracy.

Bureaucracy is one of the means by which inequality of power is maintained in our society. Bureaucracy, in public and private organisations, is growing in the same way that the power and size of wealth is growing. And it is a weapon that is used by all organisations and groups and companies wielding any power, it can be picked up by anyone and it will work for anyone; its main task is to defeat reasonableness and common sense, and replace these with the norms and values that suit the organisation using it. A perfect example is the laws/rules about secrecy. These have grown to huge proportions so that it is like a national neurosis; they always work in favour of the organisation against the individual, whilst purporting to do the opposite.

For power and wealth to move downwards in society, a battle will sometime have to be fought against bureaucracy, against the imperative of administration used against people. It is not enough to passively try to resist the growth of bureaucratic power that is felt to be somehow inevitable. We need perhaps to find an active political action **against power itself**, if we are to avoid the creeping realisation of the last century's dystopian nightmares.

This should be a part of our understanding of democracy, part of what people see as the exercise of the will of the people. At some point the question "whose land is it anyway" has to be made part of the contract between people and government, including a duty of government to uphold the interests of the people as a whole against the incursions of powerful non-governmental organisations and companies.

Many people wonder why local governments which are so happy to target independent shops with trivial or imaginary complaints, are yet unable to intervene to stop the big four retailers targeting independent shops by opening "locals" adjacent to them. Local councils are as happy to give planning permissions for this, as for the superstores they build too. Power that is not used to protect the weak, tends to help the strong against them.

Common Law

The Common Law rights of the people have steadily been eroded by statute laws. It might be time to gather Common Law together and re-state it in a legally robust form, and one that people have easy access to and can know about and understand; a new Bill of Rights, to restate and strengthen rights we already have but have forgotten, and to establish new ones where they are lacking.

Education

Since the 1980s, the nature of schools in Britain has been determined by absurd neo-Maoist educational theory which only the privileged middle classes can survive and which has in practice left many working class children struggling to even read and write properly. Behind the misleading statistics is a system that fails on even basic literacy, and British children are now half way down the world tables, due largely to the failure of disadvantaged children (Shanghai is top).

In Chairman Mao's Cultural Revolution in China the 1960s they were kicking teachers down the street as a means of destroying the past and present "knowledge elite" and creating a state of Permanent Revolution. The result was that anyone who knew anything was eradicated. It took the Chinese economy two generations to recover, and meanwhile the *power* elite stayed firmly in control. The Labour government's education advisors helped them to dismantle "presumptions" about *knowledge* and the very idea that the teacher knew things and had to impart them to the children. I advise anyone interested to read the government teacher training manuals, they have to be seen to be believed; unfortunately there is not space here to repeat their lengthy and convoluted pronouncements.

Jargon and empty phrases, complicated and perverse teacher-training techniques have undermined the ability of teachers to teach. Education in schools, according to the government approved teacher-training system, *isn't even supposed to be knowledge-based:*

"For most teachers, attending to subject knowledge content is not going to have a big outcome for pupils" *(Dylan Wiliam, author of the influential* Assessment for Learning *and, more recently, TV star).*

So now, instead of the *presumptions* about knowledge of subject, teachers have the state breathing down their necks as arbiter of what is knowledge and what isn't.

It has given us the same results as Mao's revolution gave them (before they abandoned it in favour of a conservative education system). Britain has low standards at the top end which have been dressed up as high standards. Governments' penchant for favourable statistics has led to a system built upon falsification on the deepest level.

Grade inflation has hidden the collapse of knowledge, and the consequent collapse of independent thinking in pupils that this has brought about. Lightweight pedagogic ideas, which have little basis in reality, have put teachers under rigid bureaucratic control, including trainee teachers having to regularly confirm their acceptance of the new doctrines. The system has rendered teaching in schools often incapable of preparing children for work, and has left industry short of people equipped to do the jobs available. We have school leavers, with good results on paper, unable to do simple tasks. We have, in short, a low-skill population. The inevitable result of this self-deception on a grand scale is national decline on all levels, in all areas.

One thing that is evident from our failure to compete abroad is that education fails to serve the needs of industry. But in fact it would be more accurate to say that it serves the needs of the employers of cheap *unskilled* labour, those employers who are the most powerful elements in the economy at present who, aside from cheap labour, need a population trained to passively consume, without question, what they are required to buy.

Providing vocational training in an attempt to adapt education partly to working class needs, as governments have done, is of little use when the nature of the syllabuses and of teacher-training has so deeply undermined the basic function of teaching and replaced it with state control.

The extent of the current (and it has been so for 20 years) emphasis on advertising and consumption, of a most un-analytical and passive nature, in the uniformly imposed National Curriculum, is hard to believe, but gives the game away about the direction our society and economy are taking. It shows that the mass of the population are not expected to be working in skilled jobs, but in low paid jobs, and that their position in the economy is largely as consumers, whose consumption is subsidised by government benefits, in-work and out-of-work benefits. Their usefulness is as providers of profit for large companies, and the education they receive, and the deceitful jargon it is served up to them with, betrays this fact.

What parent hasn't noticed that even in years 7-10, that is, ages 11-15, advertising and the media are the two portals of discovery through which anything from ancient history to religious education is taught? Design an advertisement for Heaven, make a poster about yourself, imagine you are a television reporter watching the battle of Hastings, etc. How may children per day are slavishly copying out trainer adverts as part of the syllabus, or taught to identify themselves and their future prospects with the media-invented so-called celebrities? The influence of our present situation is regrettably strong in schools, which are failing to provide a counter-weight to the power of media and marketing, and instead are reinforcing it. Children with little hope of employment are being taught a grotesque parody of self-confidence as a replacement for real activity. In that world, if you can't think of anything else then media studies is the default option.

A generation facing very real national decline are being cheated by being given inflated grades and empty jargon about personal ambition - a cruel trick to play on a poorly educated population destined for low paid jobs in service industries. **They are taught to be consumers in a world where products are made somewhere else.**

It is an education that spells long-term economic decline.

Meanwhile the compulsive pre-occupation with *levels* and *key-stages* has transformed teaching into a monitoring operation; bureaucracy based on assessment and measuring can give teachers, schools and parents the *impression* of precision and progress when in fact it may be a carefully managed decline.

We should also remember the origins of the measuring fetish. It was to give middle class parents the chance to move house to be next to schools higher up in "league tables". It backfired as the reports and the measuring processes were so full of set phrases that they have never given an accurate idea of the nature of the schools. How many schools are "outstanding" and "excellent"? What did it ever mean?

Britain's educational failure, with grade A* written all over it, has a huge social cost; 80% of our swollen prison population have a reading age of 11yr olds. Meanwhile employers often can't find school leavers able to do the jobs available and even universities are having to use the first year to rectify basic failings of literacy.

Aside from the miserable pointlessness of the kind of working life this whole process delivers to millions of people, it also weakens the economy, by wasting its most potentially valuable resource, the labour force.

Small Businesses and Education

Some of the problems in our education system would be partly solved by making a stronger link between industry and education. This would be one of the main tasks of an

Industrial Co-operation Board (q.v.). This has to mean that syllabuses are made to reflect, to a greater degree, the needs of employers. At the same time, this has to mean that people are trained to be more than merely low paid retail assistants and consumers, not to be uncritical consumers in an economy shaped by multinationals, but to be producers in an economy where wealth is created *and enjoyed by* everyone.

It would not just be industry therefore which would benefit from small manufacturers, for example engineering firms, being given a voice in the formation of syllabuses in schools and colleges. The practical requirements of industry would go a long way to forming schools that would serve the interests of the pupils.

It would give a better developed system of apprenticeships to link education to industry. Universities too ought to respond to the needs of industry.

We might benefit from fewer resources being spent for example on arts and media (industries where there is huge hidden unemployment) and more on training the workforce for engineering and other industries we need for exports. Personal development is about acquiring real knowledge and a skill, and can of course readily be found in sciences and engineering.

Let teachers teach

The tight grip of the National Curriculum needs to be loosened so that teachers can once again teach, and so that education can be made both broader and deeper, and freer from government control.

The so-called "traditional" methods of teaching (the disparaged "chalk and talk") allows more room for variety and spontaneity than the rigidities of the National Curriculum. It leaves room for something valuable but hard to measure, such as the accuracy that comes from a teacher's intuition or experience.

Despite the rigidities of the National Curriculum there are still stark differences between schools. In inner city areas where there is a high density of immigrants we are failing to help children sufficiently with their English. This is a matter of urgency for any child starting school, who can fall completely by the wayside. Society has to find a way of affording much smaller class sizes where children in reception, year one and year two, can be taught English to a sufficient standard before they embark upon the rest of their education. Failure in education by immigrant children is a serious social problem, which is relatively easy to deal with, but which cannot be ignored. The procedure at the moment is to have children with language difficulties in lower groups, doing easier work, which they still cannot do, all the way through primary school, setting them on a course for low achievement and failure.

Grammar schools for all who want them

Grammar school places should be available to all who want them, without any sort of test, and working class subjects ought to be properly taught in technical *and* grammar schools to prepare young people for the jobs that Britain needs in order to pay its way. There is good reason for easy movement between grammar schools and the other secondary schools.

Previous Labour governments have seen the grammar schools, in which their cabinet ministers were often educated, as part of an unfair and unequal society, and closed as many of them as they could in the 1960s, thereby depriving working class children of a route to power in their society.

To see grammar schools in this way is wilfully naive. It ignores the simple fact that there is in any society an educational elite, those who are better at academic work than others. These are the people who will hold power in a society, and who are vital to its industry and organisation and development. The only question is "What class will these people come from?" For the working classes to achieve their rightful portion of power and influence in our already unequal society, they have to have the means to reach high levels of education. The top universities in Britain are still filled disproportionately with fee paying public school boys and girls (it is not the fault of the universities but of a symptom of the failure of schools). Grammar schools are the way the working classes can rival public schools. Essentially they can get the same education as public school children but for free. We might wish that this was provided by the average comprehensive, but it just isn't so. In fact, as parents know, there is an informal hierarchy of the better state schools which are colonised by the well off who use their money to buy homes in the catchment areas; in other words they are informal private schools; *entry is reserved to the better off.* Many of the parents who use their wealth in this way are "socialists", Labour voters who strongly oppose grammar schools. If grammar schools were open to all, this queue-jumping by the rich would be defeated. If grammar schools would not require a test which too early excludes working class children who have not yet had the opportunity to develop at primary school, then they will be an instrument for equality in our society, a large-scale, long-term, door to power for the working classes.

You can't make a social revolution by cutting off the route to power before those at the bottom have got there, nor by pretending there is no top. At present the top is held by the middle classes.

Why have grammar schools at all?

To bring about a lowering of educational standards at the top in a misguided bid to bring about equality by *levelling down* is a serious mistake. It doesn't help the working classes to lower academic standards at Oxford and Cambridge for example. It *does* help the working classes to make the best schools available to anyone who wants them, so that potentially academically talented children of all classes can get the education they need to get them to the top universities, and thereby into the top positions of power and influence. The struggle for equality and power is not a game, and it is not a need that can be satisfied by statistics, quotas and targets, nor by moving the goalposts nearer. And certainly not by pretending that inequalities don't exist. When they no longer exist, *then* we can say they don't exist.

If we don't have grammar schools the country will continue to be run by public schoolboys.

Crime and punishment
Gangs.

Social poverty is as devastating as material poverty. In some areas, for example, it is commonplace for children to be afraid *not* to join a gang. The very serious crime problem in Britain, most of which is swept under the carpet as "low level crime", cannot be finally dealt with unless the police force is a community-based body, not the arm of the state it has partly become. We should significantly extend the size and powers of the Community Police Force, and bring a return to beat policing. Police forces need to be governed in small units by locally elected bodies to ensure that they respond to the needs of housing estates and other communities. Middle class Labour voters are often loath to contemplate the facts of what society is really like for the poor, partly because they are afraid of what measures would be required to deal with it.

Prison.

The prison population has grown 900% since 1931 (the UK population has grown only 40%). The crime rate has soared somewhere past 5 million crimes per year. Moral loosening and decline is one reason; it's easy to see for example that children are too often taught that they can and should do as they please - until finally they are locked up in prison. The other cause is hopeless poverty. It is the worst educated and least intelligent who fill our prisons.

People argue about whether crime is a social or a moral problem - but it is both. Long term material poverty easily breeds social and moral poverty.

When successive generations are left with no hope of escape from poverty and unemployment, then misery and despair follow.

Most middle class people would admit to knowing little of what horrors greet those who go to prison. Fewer would admit to knowing little of the misery of everyday poverty outside prison, for millions of Britons.

The law and its enforcement cannot alone reduce crime - there has to be a morality too, a sense of right and wrong and consideration for others. But hypocrisy is a poor moral teacher. In a society that has abandoned itself to greed and where millions are left to hopeless poverty, and where their own party has forgotten about them, there is little the poor can hope for; and without hope there is despair and moral and personal collapse. That is now built into our society and the middle class left are adept at walking past it without seeing it, morally scared of what it is, and what it means.

Part of public morality has to include a fair sharing-out of the material wealth. Without that, talk of conscience or consideration for others is shallow and unconvincing. In other words, morality cannot be separated from politics. When we have politics that acknowledges the right of every individual to a fair share of the pie, *then* we can expect a morality based on solidarity and consideration for others and.

There are many things wrong with the prisons and justice system that can be adjusted; sentencing, conditions in the prisons themselves, wrongly given parole, lack of rehabilitation etc. The most glaring fault of prisons is that they are not free from crime, but are instead filled with violence and corruption and drugs. Does the state have the right to incarcerate anyone if it cannot protect them from crime? Cameron is right when he resists the soft/hard labels. But in the long term the crime problem which blights so many people's lives cannot be solved until grinding poverty and suffering, and gross inequality, is removed from our society.

An Underclass

Beneath the millions of poor who struggle along on subsistence wages is a growing underclass who, despite the availability of benefits, live beyond the reach of morality or hope. There is no vision of the future for them for there are no suitable jobs because the economy has told itself it doesn't need them, and the education system has left them almost illiterate. For them the days are filled with anything from idleness or television to drugs, to violence and abuse. They are not on the political map. They do not count. The middle class left tend to despise people in this wretched condition for the very depravity it creates, seeing no fault in an economy which is designed to exclude a whole class who might otherwise be young, strong working people.

A working class movement has to have solidarity with the weak, the oppressed, and with the wretched and the unworthy. And that cannot mean only by arranging for hand-outs, benefits, soup, charity and social workers to pick up the ugly mess. It has to mean organising society and the economy 1) to include the contribution they can make and 2) to give them an equal share of the pie.

The Present and the Future

An economy which increasingly relies on a small elite in banks to generate money for imports through its investments of the fruits of other peoples labour, is one built on inequality and cynicism- and waste. As we have seen, it is a fragile structure with parasites at the top and unwanted passengers on the bottom, which cannot last in the long term. Can we really face a future based on such a sordid arrangement? Throughout the past decades we have stretched ourselves about as far as this miserable vision of society will go. The result is a depressing and degraded society based largely on infantilism and poverty. We need a future where we are less gullible and less cynical at the same time. It isn't enough to blindly blame "politicians" for what are our own faults. We can blame our *politics*, but that is not the same thing. Our politics lacks any vision of a future free from poverty. It is time we stopped allowing ourselves to have our awareness fed to us by television and the press. We need to think for ourselves. We need to have sufficient maturity to demand greater equality.

Changes to the Constitution?

A monarchy or a republic?

If Britain were to change to a republic today, there is little doubt whose republic it would be - it would be a middle class republic. In fact nothing would more gratify the middle classes who have hijacked the Labour movement, than if the monarchy were to be abolished, as it represents a rival to their power and influence. The main difficulty in creating a presidency or similar office would be how to create one that had no political power to limit the power of the people as expressed through the sovereignty of Parliament. At present we already have that sort of constricted office, in the monarchy, and it is hard to see how that aspect could be improved upon by a presidential system. (We might though look at the way ministers are using Royal Prerogative in their dealings with the EU for example). It is hard to imagine a British monarch attempting to impede the power of the people as expressed in Parliament (The Queen didn't even refuse to allow the unconstitutional delegation of British Sovereignty to a foreign power, the EU, which was illegal and technically treason).

An *elected* president would have political power by virtue of being elected, and we would drift towards a presidential system of government as in the USA, where Parliament is overwhelmed by the presidential prerogative, and elections are the media spectacle of a two-man battle.

An *appointed* president, a more or less symbolic Head of State, like the monarch, would inevitably have to be either an ex-politician (i.e. previous prime ministers/ministers whom we had rejected at the ballot box), or other worthy or powerful or influential people, in other words a gateway to corruption (the kind of corruption which afflicts the French Presidency).

The *dis*advantage of the monarchy is the extent to which it is the head of an aristocratic beast, and thereby promotes ideas of inequality of rank. However, the most potent hierarchy in our society is the one which gives the middle classes control of the media, politics, and education, and the one which ensures that all the money stays with those huge entities that already have it. The aristocracy is a beast which is still partly alive and it still has influence and ownership. However, it is doubtful whether weakening the small aristocratic element of the hugely powerful capitalist class would be anything more than a distraction. In fact its removal would directly benefit the middle classes, who would inherit their power. What is vital is to challenge and check the influence of the multinational corporations. There is enough reason to believe that the principal figures of our monarchy are as likely to feel more loyalty to their own country and people, from whom they take their power and identity, than to that nameless giant who dwarfs even them. We know more or less where we've got the royals, - the shifting sands of a presidency might not be so predictable and ought to be approached with extreme caution.

Sharing out the Pie

For too long, middle class parties have only been able to imagine helping the poor by providing benefits, with little thought of equality through wages. It is time to share out the pie more fairly.

A working class movement must have as its priority to end poverty and its resulting misery once and for all.

A Working Class Alternative To Labour

"   ....The man who is employed for wages is as much a business man as his employer;

the attorney in a country town is as much a business man as the corporation council in a giant metropolis;

the merchant in a crossroads store is as much a business man as the merchant in New York;

the farmer who goes forth in the morning and toils all day, who begins in the spring and toils all summer and who is by the application of his brain and muscle to the natural resources of the country creates wealth, is as much a business man as the man who goes upon the board of trade and bets upon the price of grain;

the miners who go down a thousand feet in the earth
or climb two thousand feet on the cliffs
and bring forth from their hiding places
the precious metals
to be poured in the channels of
trade,

are as much businessmen as the few financial magnates
who
in a back room
corner the money of the world."

(John Dos Passos, "USA")

Appendix

How the proposed minimum wage was calculated:

the figure of £9,30 was worked out thus;

Family of 4 need per month/ (single parent family in brackets{based on 1parent +2children})

First; to scrape by, a basic minimum;

Rent/ mortgage £700 (£600) (London £1400)

Council tax £150 (£150)

Fuel £150 (£125)

Insurance £50 (£50)

Telephone 350 (£35)

Food £725 (£580)

Car

insurance and petrol £100 (£90)

tax £20 (£20)

MOT £10 (£10)

repairs £30 (£30)

School meals £120 (£120)

TV license £15 (£15)

Misc, Entertainment etc £100 (£75)

clothes £50 (£35)

Total £2275 (£1845) (London £2975)

= £27,000pa (£22,140pa) (London £35,700)

if 2 are working this needs £13,650pa each (London £17,850)

= £262pwk each (London £343)

<u>= £6.50 phr</u> (London £8.58)

This leaves ....   which would cost x to provide per month; (single-parent family in brackets)

No holidays £200 (£170)

No spare cash at all £200 (£170)

No toys £50 (£50)

No outings £50 (£50)

No expensive repairs £150 (£140)

No journeys £100 (£80)

No capital EVER £200 (£160)

Total £950 (£820)

Which is;

An extra £2.70 per hour each (Single parent needs £9.30 phr + £1053benefits, plus child care costs)

£6.50+£2.70=£9.20) (London £8.55+£2.70=£11.28)

To this I add en extra 10p per hr. = £9.30 (London £11.38)

So to summarize; I have *started* by working out a figure for basic needs, which interestingly gave almost precisely the same as the government figure for their minimum wage. This means 2 people work full time and just about manage to get their basic requirements, provided they *never* have any other costs, nothing breaks, nothing happens and your house is already fully equipped with everything you will ever need. In real life such calculations are totally unrealistic, and anyone earning that would within short time be either in debt or unable to meet their obligations and requirements.

I have then added a monthly sum based on reasonable expectations for a family of 4 (and separately also for a single parent family). These figures are based on realistic expectations for a life that is not one of poverty, and for an income that will not *in the long run result in poverty.* Current minimum wage levels are more or less set at levels that would be possible for one or two weeks only, not for a lifetime. The expenses here are things which would enable people to provide properly, to plan long and short term for their families, even to benefit from the economies that brings. These are things which are at present the privilege of the middle classes. There is no reason why that should be, and the real cost of the shortfall in these expenses is anyway later picked up by the state. It represents the difference between a decent life, which can be both interesting and constructive, and with a degree of self respect - and one of grinding poverty in work.

The figure of £19,400 (London £23,673) is approximately 80% of the median national income(£24,000). It would be the highest minimum wage in Europe, Luxembourg has £8.80) (calculated as either an absolute sum or as a percentage of the median). It would effectively eradicate *most* poverty from Britain.

Printed in England